THE YALE SHAKESPEARE

Revised Edition

———————

General Editors

Helge Kökeritz and Charles T. Prouty

———————

Published on the fund

given to the Yale University Press in 1917

by the members of the

Kingsley Trust Association

(Scroll and Key Society of Yale College)

to commemorate the seventy-fifth anniversary

of the founding of the society

THE YALE SHAKESPEARE

AS YOU LIKE IT

Edited by S. C. Burchell

NEW HAVEN: YALE UNIVERSITY PRESS

London: Oxford University Press

FIRST PUBLISHED, OCTOBER, 1919
REVISED EDITION, FEBRUARY, 1954

Preface of the General Editors

AS the late Professor Tucker Brooke has observed, practically all modern editions of Shakespeare are 18th-century versions of the plays, based on the additions, alterations, and emendations of editors of that period. It has been our purpose, as it was Professor Brooke's, to give the modern reader Shakespeare's plays in the approximate form of their original appearance.

About half the plays appeared in quarto form before the publication of the First Folio in 1623. Thus for a large number of plays the only available text is that of the Folio. In the case of quarto plays our policy has been to use that text as the basis of the edition, unless it is clear that the text has been contaminated.

Interesting for us today is the fact that there are no act or scene divisions in the Quartos with the exception of *Othello*, which does mark Acts I, II, IV, and V but lacks indications of scenes. Even in the Folio, although act divisions are generally noted, only a part of the scenes are divided. In no case, either in Quarto or Folio, is there any indication of the place of action. The manifold scene divisions for the battle in such a play as *Antony and Cleopatra*, together with such locations as "Another part of the field," are the additions of the 18th century.

We have eliminated all indications of the place and time of action, because there is no authority for them in the originals and because Shakespeare gives such information, when it is requisite for understanding the play, through the dialogue of the actors. We have been sparing in our use of added scene and, in some cases, act divisions, because these frequently impede the flow of the action, which in Shakespeare's time was curiously like that of modern films.

Spelling has been modernized except when the original clearly indicates a pronunciation unlike our own, e.g. *desart* (desert), *divel* (devil), *banket* (banquet), and often in such Elizabethan syncopations as *stolne* (stol'n), and *tane* (ta'en). In reproducing such forms we have followed the inconsistent usage of the original.

We have also preserved the original capitalization when this is a part of the meaning. In like manner we have tended to adopt the lineation of the original in many cases where modern editors print prose as verse or verse as prose. We have, moreover, followed the original punctuation wherever it was practicable.

In verse we print a final -*ed* to indicate its full syllabic value, otherwise '*d*. In prose we have followed the inconsistencies of the original in this respect.

Our general practice has been to include in footnotes all information a reader needs for immediate understanding of the given page. In somewhat empiric fashion we repeat glosses as we think the reader needs to be reminded of the meaning. Further information is given in notes (indicated by the letter *N* in the footnotes) to be found at the back of each volume. Appendices deal with the text and sources of the play.

Square brackets indicate material not found in the original text. Long emendations or lines taken from another authoritative text of a play are indicated in the footnotes for the information of the reader. We have silently corrected obvious typographical errors.

CONTENTS

[THE ACTORS' NAMES

DUKE SENIOR, *living in exile in the Forest of Arden*
DUKE FREDERICK, *his brother and usurper of the dukedom*
AMIENS
JAQUES } *lords attending on the banished Duke*
LE BEAU, *a courtier attending on Duke Frederick*
CHARLES, *wrestler to Duke Frederick*
OLIVER
JAQUES DE BOYS } *sons of Sir Rowland de Boys*
ORLANDO
ADAM
DENNIS } *servants to Oliver*
TOUCHSTONE, *a clown*
SIR OLIVER MARTEXT, *a vicar*
CORIN
SILVIUS } *shepherds*
WILLIAM, *a country fellow in love with Audrey*
HYMEN

ROSALIND, *daughter to the banished Duke*
CELIA, *daughter to Duke Frederick*
PHEBE, *a shepherdess*
AUDREY, *a country wench*
Lords, Pages, Foresters, Attendants]

Act I

SCENE 1

Enter Orlando and Adam.

Orlando. As I remember, Adam, it was upon this
fashion: he bequeathed me by will but poor a thousand crowns and, as thou say'st, charged my brother
on his blessing to breed me well; and there begins my
sadness. My brother Jaques he keeps at school, and
report speaks goldenly of his profit. For my part, he
keeps me rustically at home, or—to speak more
properly—stays me here at home unkept, for call
you that keeping for a gentleman of my birth that
differs not from the stalling of an ox? His horses are
bred better; for, besides that they are fair with their
feeding, they are taught their manage, and to that
end riders dearly hir'd. But I, his brother, gain nothing under him but growth, for the which his animals
on his dunghills are as much bound to him as I. Besides this nothing that he so plentifully gives me,
the something that nature gave me, his countenance
seems to take from me. He lets me feed with his
hinds, bars me the place of a brother and, as much

2 he N. (N refers throughout to the corresponding note given at
the end of the text.) poor a a miserable. 4 breed raise. 5 school
college. 6 goldenly glowingly. 7 rustically like a peasant. 8 stays
keeps. unkept uncared for. 12 manage training paces. 13 dearly
expensively. 17 countenance behavior. 19 hinds field servants.

1

as in him lies, mines my gentility with my education.
This is it, Adam, that grieves me and the spirit of
my father, which I think is within me, begins to
mutiny against this servitude. I will no longer endure it, though yet I know no wise remedy how to
avoid it.

Enter Oliver.

Adam. Yonder comes my master, your brother.   26

Orlando. Go apart, Adam, and thou shalt hear how
he will shake me up.

Oliver. Now, sir, what make you here?   29

Orlando. Nothing. I am not taught to make anything.

Oliver. What mar you then, sir?

Orlando. Marry, sir, I am helping you to mar that
which God made, a poor unworthy brother of yours,
with idleness.   35

Oliver. Marry, sir, be better employed, and be
naught a while.

Orlando. Shall I keep your hogs and eat husks with
them? What prodigal portion have I spent that I
should come to such penury?   40

Oliver. Know you where you are, sir?

Orlando. O, sir, very well. Here in your orchard.

Oliver. Know you before whom, sir?

Orlando. Ay, better than him I am before knows
me. I know you are my eldest brother, and in the
gentle condition of blood you should so know me.

20 **mines** undermines. 29 **make you** are you doing. 32 **mar** N. 36
Marry contraction of 'by the Virgin Mary.' **be naught** keep quiet.
39 **prodigal portion** N. 41 **where** in whose presence (Orlando takes
the literal meaning). 44 **Ay** F *I* (F is the First Folio of 1623). 46
gentle condition of blood natural kindness of our relationship.

The courtesy of nations allows you my better, in that you are the first born, but the same tradition takes not away my blood, were there twenty brothers betwixt us. I have as much of my father in me as you, albeit I confess your coming before me is nearer to his reverence.

Oliver. What, boy!

Orlando. Come, come, elder brother, you are too young in this.   55

Oliver. Wilt thou lay hands on me, villain?

Orlando. I am no villain; I am the youngest son of Sir Rowland de Boys. He was my father, and he is thrice a villain that says such a father begot villains. Wert thou not my brother, I would not take this hand from thy throat till this other had pull'd out thy tongue for saying so. Thou hast rail'd on thyself.

Adam. Sweet masters, be patient. For your father's remembrance, be at accord.   65

Oliver. Let me go, I say!

Orlando. I will not till I please; you shall hear me. My father charg'd you in his will to give me good education. You have train'd me like a peasant, obscuring and hiding from me all gentleman-like qualities. The spirit of my father grows strong in me, and I will no longer endure it. Therefore allow me such exercises as may become a gentleman, or give me the poor allottery my father left me by testament. With that I will go buy my fortunes.   75

Oliver. And what wilt thou do? Beg when that is spent? Well, sir, get you in. I will not long be trou-

47 courtesy of nations conventions of civilized society. 52 reverence N. 55 young brash. 56 villain N. 73 exercises occupations. 74 allottery share.

3

bled with you; you shall have some part of your will.
I pray you, leave me. 79

Orlando. I will no further offend you than becomes
me for my good.

Oliver. Get you with him, you old dog.

Adam. Is 'old dog' my reward? Most true, I have
lost my teeth in your service. God be with my old
master. He would not have spoke such a word. 85

Exeunt Orlando, Adam.

Oliver. Is it even so? Begin you to grow upon me?
I will physic your rankness, and yet give no thousand crowns neither. Holla, Dennis!

Enter Dennis.

Dennis. Calls your worship? 89

Oliver. Was not Charles, the Duke's wrastler, here
to speak with me?

Dennis. So please you, he is here at the door and
importunes access to you.

Oliver. Call him in. [*Exit Dennis.*] 'Twill be a good
way, and tomorrow the wrastling is. 95

Enter Charles.

Charles. Good morrow to your worship.

Oliver. Good Monsieur Charles, what's the new news
at the new court?

Charles. There's no news at the court, sir, but the
old news: that is, the old Duke is banished by his
younger brother, the new Duke, and three or four
loving lords have put themselves into voluntary exile
with him, whose lands and revenues enrich the new
Duke. Therefore he gives them good leave to wander.

86 **grow** presume. 87 **physic** purge. **rankness** insolence, foulness.
90 **wrastler** N. 97 **Monsieur** N.

Oliver. Can you tell if Rosalind, the Duke's daughter, be banished with her father? 106

Charles. O, no. For the Duke's daughter, her cousin, so loves her, being ever from their cradles bred together, that she would have followed her exile, or have died to stay behind her. She is at the court and no less beloved of her uncle than his own daughter, and never two ladies loved as they do.

Oliver. Where will the old Duke live?

Charles. They say he is already in the Forest of Arden, and a many merry men with him. And there they live like the old Robin Hood of England. They say many young gentlemen flock to him every day and fleet the time carelessly as they did in the golden world. 119

Oliver. What, you wrastle tomorrow before the new Duke?

Charles. Marry, do I, sir. And I came to acquaint you with a matter: I am given, sir, secretly to understand that your younger brother Orlando hath a disposition to come in disguis'd against me to try a fall. Tomorrow, sir, I wrastle for my credit, and he that escapes me without some broken limb shall acquit him well. Your brother is but young and tender, and for your love I would be loath to foil him, as I must for my own honor if he come in. Therefore, out of my love to you, I came hither to acquaint you withal, that either you might stay him from his intendment or brook such disgrace well as he shall run into; in that it is a thing of his own search, and altogether against my will. 135

Oliver. Charles, I thank thee for thy love to me,

114 Forest of Arden N. 118 fleet pass. golden world N. 129 **loath** unwilling. foil throw. 132 **withal** with this. intendment intent. 133 brook . . . well endure.

which thou shalt find I will most kindly requite. I
had myself notice of my brother's purpose herein,
and have by underhand means labored to dissuade
him from it; but he is resolute. I'll tell thee, Charles,
it is the stubbornest young fellow of France—full of
ambition, an envious emulator of every man's good
parts, a secret and villainous contriver against me,
his natural brother. Therefore use thy discretion;
I had as lief thou didst break his neck as his finger.
And thou wert best look to 't; for if thou dost him
any slight disgrace, or if he do not mightily grace
himself on thee, he will practise against thee by poison, entrap thee by some treacherous device, and
never leave thee till he hath tane thy life by some
indirect means or other. For I assure thee—and
almost with tears I speak it—there is not one so
young and so villainous this day living. I speak but
brotherly of him; but should I anatomize him to
thee as he is, I must blush and weep, and thou must
look pale and wonder.   156

Charles. I am heartily glad I came hither to you.
If he come tomorrow, I'll give him his payment. If
ever he go alone again, I'll never wrastle for prize
more. And so God keep your worship. *Exit.*   160

[*Oliver.*] Farewell, good Charles. Now will I stir
this gamester. I hope I shall see an end of him, for
my soul—yet I know not why—hates nothing more
than he. Yet he's gentle, never school'd and yet
learned, full of noble device, of all sorts enchantingly

139 underhand unobtrusive. 144 **natural brother** blood brother.
145 **had as lief** had as soon. 146 **wert best** had better. **look to 't**
take care. 147 **grace** do credit to. 148 **practise** scheme. 150 **tane**
taken. 154 **anatomize** analyze. 159 **go alone** walk without aid.
161 **stir** incite. 162 **gamester** athlete. 165 **device** purpose. **sorts**
types of people. **enchantingly** as if by enchantment.

beloved, and indeed so much in the heart of the world and especially of my own people who best know him, that I am altogether misprised. But it shall not be so long; this wrastler shall clear all. Nothing remains but that I kindle the boy thither, which now I'll go about. *Exit.* 171

SCENE 2

Enter Rosalind and Celia.

Celia. I pray thee, Rosalind, sweet my coz, be merry.

Rosalind. Dear Celia, I show more mirth than I am mistress of, and would you yet I were merrier? Unless you could teach me to forget a banished father, you must not learn me how to remember any extraordinary pleasure. 7

Celia. Herein I see thou lov'st me not with the full weight that I love thee. If my uncle, thy banished father, had banished thy uncle, the Duke my father, so thou hadst been still with me, I could have taught my love to take thy father for mine; so wouldst thou, if the truth of thy love to me were so righteously temper'd as mine is to thee. 14

Rosalind. Well, I will forget the condition of my estate to rejoice in yours.

Celia. You know my father hath no child but I, nor none is like to have. And truly, when he dies, thou shalt be his heir; for what he hath taken away from

168 **misprised** despised. 169 **clear all** settle everything. 170 **kindle . . . thither** incite him to challenge the wrestler. 1 **coz** cousin. 4 I F omits. 6 **learn me** instruct me. 11 **so** provided that. 13 **righteously temper'd** thoroughly consistent. 16 **estate** fortune.

thy father perforce I will render thee again in affection. By mine honor, I will. And when I break that oath, let me turn monster. Therefore, my sweet Rose, my dear Rose, be merry.

Rosalind. From henceforth I will, coz, and devise sports. Let me see. What think you of falling in love? 26

Celia. Marry, I prithee do, to make sport withal. But love no man in good earnest, nor no further in sport neither than with safety of a pure blush thou mayst in honor come off again. 30

Rosalind. What shall be our sport then?

Celia. Let us sit and mock the good housewife Fortune from her wheel, that her gifts may henceforth be bestowed equally. 34

Rosalind. I would we could do so, for her benefits are mightily misplaced and the bountiful blind woman doth most mistake in her gifts to women.

Celia. 'Tis true. For those that she makes fair she scarce makes honest, and those that she makes honest she makes very ill-favoredly. 40

Rosalind. Nay, now thou goest from Fortune's office to Nature's. Fortune reigns in gifts of the world, not in the lineaments of Nature.

Enter Clown [Touchstone].

Celia. No? When Nature hath made a fair creature, may she not by Fortune fall into the fire? Though Nature hath given us wit to flout at Fortune, hath not Fortune sent in this fool to cut off the argument?

20 **perforce** by force. 25 **sports** amusements. 27 **prithee** pray you; F *prethee*. 29 **with . . . blush** with modesty. 30 **come off** escape. 32 **housewife Fortune** N. 39 **honest** virtuous. 40 **ill-favoredly** ugly looking. 41 **office** function. 43 **Nature** N.

Rosalind. Indeed there is Fortune too hard for Nature, when Fortune makes Nature's natural the cutter-off of Nature's wit.   51

Celia. Peradventure this is not Fortune's work neither but Nature's, who perceiveth our natural wits too dull to reason of such goddesses and hath sent this natural for our whetstone. For always the dullness of the fool is the whetstone of the wits. How now, wit? Whether wander you?

Touchstone. Mistress, you must come away to your father.

Celia. Were you made the messenger?   60

Touchstone. No, by mine honor, but I was bid to come for you.

Rosalind. Where learned you that oath, fool?

Touchstone. Of a certain knight, that swore by his honor they were good pancakes and swore by his honor the mustard was naught. Now I'll stand to it, the pancakes were naught and the mustard was good. And yet was not the knight forsworn.

Celia. How prove you that in the great heap of your knowledge?   70

Rosalind. Ay, marry, now unmuzzle your wisdom.

Touchstone. Stand you both forth now. Stroke your chins and swear by your beards that I am a knave.

Celia. By our beards—if we had them—thou art.

Touchstone. By my knavery—if I had it—then I were. But if you swear by that that is not, you are not forsworn. No more was this knight swearing by his honor, for he never had any; or, if he had, he had sworn it away before ever he saw those pancakes or that mustard.   80

50 natural idiot. 54 reason of discuss. and F omits. 55 whetstone N. 57 whether whither. 66 naught worthless. stand to it maintain. 68 was . . . forsworn did not swear falsely.

Celia. Prithee, who is't that thou mean'st?

Touchstone. One that old Frederick, your father, loves.

Celia. My father's love is enough to honor him enough. Speak no more of him. You'll be whipt for taxation one of these days. 86

Touchstone. The more pity that fools may not speak wisely what wise men do foolishly.

Celia. By my troth, thou sayest true; for, since the little wit that fools have was silenced, the little foolery that wise men have makes a great show. Here comes Monsieur Le Beau.

Enter Le Beau.

Rosalind. With his mouth full of news.

Celia. Which he will put on us as pigeons feed their young. 95

Rosalind. Then shall we be news-cramm'd.

Celia. All the better; we shall be the more marketable. *Bon jour*, Monsieur Le Beau, what's the news?

Le Beau. Fair Princess, you have lost much good sport. 100

Celia. Sport? Of what color?

Le Beau. What color, madam? How shall I answer you?

Rosalind. As wit and fortune will.

Touchstone. Or as the Destinies decree. 105

Celia. Well said. That was laid on with a trowel.

Touchstone. Nay, if I keep not my rank.

Rosalind. Thou losest thy old smell.

84 Celia N. 85 enough N. 86 **taxation** insolent criticism, slander. 89 **troth** faith. 94 **put on** force on. 97 **marketable** plumper and therefore more valuable. 98 **Bon jour** N. 101 **color** sort. 108 **smell** N.

Le Beau. You amaze me, ladies. I would have told you of good wrastling, which you have lost the sight of. 111

Rosalind. Yet tell us the manner of the wrastling.

Le Beau. I will tell you the beginning, and if it please your ladyships, you may see the end; for the best is yet to do. And here where you are they are coming to perform it. 116

Celia. Well, the beginning that is dead and buried.

Le Beau. There comes an old man and his three sons.

Celia. I could match this beginning with an old tale. 121

Le Beau. Three proper young men of excellent growth and presence.

Rosalind. With bills on their necks: 'Be it known unto all men by these presents.' 125

Le Beau. The eldest of the three wrastled with Charles, the Duke's wrastler; which Charles in a moment threw him and broke three of his ribs, that there is little hope of life in him. So he serv'd the second, and so the third. Yonder they lie, the poor old man their father making such pitiful dole over them that all the beholders take his part with weeping.

Rosalind. Alas! 134

Touchstone. But what is the sport, Monsieur, that the ladies have lost?

Le Beau. Why, this that I speak of.

Touchstone. Thus men may grow wiser every day. It is the first time that ever I heard breaking of ribs was sport for ladies. 140

109 **amaze** perplex. 115 **to do** to be done. 120 **old tale** N. 122 **proper** admirable. 123 **presence** carriage. 124 **bills** signs. 125 **presents** N. 127 **which** N. 128 **that** so that. 131 **dole** lamentation.

Celia. Or I, I promise thee.

Rosalind. But is there any else longs to see this
broken music in his sides? Is there yet another dotes
upon rib-breaking? Shall we see this wrastling,
cousin?   145

Le Beau. You must if you stay here; for here is the
place appointed for the wrastling, and they are
ready to perform it.

Celia. Yonder sure they are coming. Let us now
stay and see it.   150

*Flourish. Enter Duke [Frederick], Lords, Orlando,
Charles, and Attendants.*

Duke. Come on. Since the youth will not be entreated, his own peril on his forwardness.

Rosalind. Is yonder the man?

Le Beau. Even he, madam.   154

Celia. Alas, he is too young; yet he looks successfully.

Duke. How now, daughter and cousin, are you
crept hither to see the wrastling?

Rosalind. Ay, my liege, so please you give us leave.

Duke. You will take little delight in it, I can tell
you. There is such odds in the man. In pity of the
challenger's youth I would fain dissuade him, but he
will not be entreated. Speak to him, ladies; see if you
can move him.   164

Celia. Call him hether, good Monsieur Le Beau.

Duke. Do so. I'll not be by.

Le Beau. Monsieur the Challenger, the princess
calls for you.

142. **any** anyone. **longs** who longs. 143 **broken music** N. 151
entreated persuaded. 152 **forwardness** foolhardiness. 155 **looks
successfully** seems able to succeed. 161 **such . . . man** N. 162
fain be glad to. 165 **hether** N.

Orlando. I attend them with all respect and duty.

Rosalind. Young man, have you challeng'd Charles the Wrastler? 171

Orlando. No, fair princess, he is the general challenger. I come but in as others do, to try with him the strength of my youth. 174

Celia. Young gentleman, your spirits are too bold for your years. You have seen cruel proof of this man's strength. If you saw yourself with your eyes or knew yourself with your judgment, the fear of your adventure would counsel you to a more equal enterprise. We pray you for your own sake to embrace your own safety and give over this attempt.

Rosalind. Do, young sir. Your reputation shall not therefore be misprised. We will make it our suit to the Duke that the wrastling might not go forward.

Orlando. I beseech you, punish me not with your hard thoughts, wherein I confess me much guilty to deny so fair and excellent ladies anything. But let your fair eyes and gentle wishes go with me to my trial; wherein if I be foil'd, there is but one sham'd that was never gracious; if kill'd, but one dead that is willing to be so. I shall do my friends no wrong, for I have none to lament me; the world no injury, for in it I have nothing. Only in the world I fill up a place, which may be better supplied when I have made it empty. 195

Rosalind. The little strength that I have, I would it were with you.

Celia. And mine to eke out hers.

Rosalind. Fare you well. Pray heaven I be deceiv'd in you. 200

---

169 them N. 183 **misprised** despised. **suit** petition. 190 **gracious** in good favor. 199 **deceiv'd in** mistaken about (i.e. his strength).

13

Celia. Your heart's desires be with you.

Charles. Come, where is this young gallant that is so desirous to lie with his mother earth?

Orlando. Ready, sir; but his will hath in it a more modest working. 205

Duke. You shall try but one fall.

Charles. No, I warrant your grace you shall not entreat him to a second, that have so mightily per-suaded him from a first. 209

Orlando. You mean to mock me after; you should not have mock'd me before. But come your ways.

Rosalind. Now Hercules be thy speed, young man.

Celia. I would I were invisible, to catch the strong fellow by the leg. [*Charles and Orlando*] *Wrastle.*

Rosalind. O excellent young man! 215

Celia. If I had a thunderbolt in mine eye, I can tell who should down. [*Charles is thrown.*] *Shout.*

Duke. No more, no more.

Orlando. Yes, I beseech your grace; I am not yet well breath'd. 220

Duke. How dost thou, Charles?

Le Beau. He cannot speak, my lord.

Duke. Bear him away. What is thy name, young man?

Orlando. Orlando, my liege, the youngest son of Sir Rowland de Boys. 226

Duke. I would thou hadst been son to some man else.

The world esteem'd thy father honorable,

But I did find him still mine enemy. 229

205 **modest working** moderate intention. 212 **Hercules be thy speed** May Hercules give you good fortune. 220 **well breath'd** fully exercised. 227 **some man else** some other man. 229 **still** always.

14

Thou should'st have better pleas'd me with this deed,
Hadst thou descended from another house.
But fare thee well; thou art a gallant youth.
I would thou hadst told me of another father.

        Exeunt Duke, [Le Beau, and Lords].

  Celia. Were I my father, coz, would I do this?   234
  Orlando. I am more proud to be Sir Rowland's son,
His youngest son, and would not change that calling
To be adopted heir to Frederick.
  Rosalind. My father lov'd Sir Rowland as his soul,
And all the world was of my father's mind.
Had I before known this young man his son,   240
I should have given him tears unto entreaties,
Ere he should thus have ventur'd.
  Celia.   Gentle cousin,
Let us go thank him and encourage him.
My father's rough and envious disposition
Sticks me at heart. Sir, you have well deserv'd.   245
If you do keep your promises in love
But justly as you have exceeded all promise,
Your mistress shall be happy.
  Rosalind [presenting a locket]. Gentleman,
Wear this for me, one out of suits with fortune   249
That could give more, but that her hand lacks means.
Shall we go, coz?
  Celia.   Ay; fare you well, fair gentleman.
  Orlando. Can I not say 'I thank you'? My better
      parts
Are all thrown down, and that which here stands up
Is but a quintain, a mere lifeless block.

233 **thou hadst** to be read 'thou'dst.' 236 **calling** name. 241 **unto**
in addition to. 245 **Sticks me at heart** stabs me in the heart.
247 **But justly** as exactly. 249 **out of suits** out of favor N. 252
parts qualities. 254 **quintain** N.

Rosalind. He calls us back. My pride fell with my
    fortunes. 255

I'll ask him what he would. Did you call, sir?
Sir, you have wrastled well and overthrown
More than your enemies.
    Celia.   Will you go, coz?
    Rosalind. Have with you. Fare you well.   *Exeunt.*
    Orlando. What passion hangs these weights upon
    my tongue? 260

I cannot speak to her, yet she urg'd conference.

Enter Le Beau.

O poor Orlando, thou art overthrown;
Or Charles or something weaker masters thee.
    Le Beau. Good sir, I do in friendship counsel you
To leave this place. Albeit you have deserv'd 265
High commendation, true applause, and love,
Yet such is now the Duke's condition
That he misconsters all that you have done.
The Duke is humorous. What he is indeed
More suits you to conceive than I to speak of. 270
    Orlando. I thank you, sir. And pray you, tell me
    this:

Which of the two was daughter of the Duke,
That here was at the wrastling?
    Le Beau. Neither his daughter, if we judge by man-
    ners.

But yet indeed the taller is his daughter. 275
The other is daughter to the banish'd Duke
And here detain'd by her usurping uncle

---

259 **Have with you** I'm coming with you. 260 **passion** a strong
emotion. 261 **urg'd conference** invited conversation. 267 **condition** mood. 268 **misconsters** misconstrues. 269 **humorous** temperamental N. 275 **taller** N. 276 **other is** to be read 'other's.'

To keep his daughter company, whose loves
Are dearer than the natural bond of sisters.
But I can tell you that of late this Duke   280
Hath tane displeasure 'gainst his gentle niece,
Grounded upon no other argument
But that the people praise her for her virtues,
And pity her for her good father's sake.
And, on my life, his malice 'gainst the lady   285
Will suddenly break forth. Sir, fare you well.
Hereafter, in a better world than this,
I shall desire more love and knowledge of you.
   Orlando. I rest much bounden to you. Fare you
    well.   *[Exit Le Beau.]*
Thus must I from the smoke into the smother,   290
From tyrant Duke unto a tyrant brother.
But heavenly Rosalind!   *Exit.*

SCENE 3

Enter Celia and Rosalind.

Celia. Why, cousin, why, Rosalind! Cupid have
mercy, not a word?
   Rosalind. Not one to throw at a dog.
   Celia. No, thy words are too precious to be cast
away upon curs; throw some of them at me. Come,
lame me with reasons.   6
   Rosalind. Then there were two cousins laid up,
when the one should be lam'd with reasons and the
other mad without any.

281 **tane** taken. 282 **argument** cause. 289 **bounden** obligated.
290 **from . . . smother** 'out of the frying pan into the fire.' SD
Rosalind N. (SD is used throughout to indicate stage direction.)
8 reasons N.

Celia. But is all this for your father?　　　　　　　　1

Rosalind. No, some of it is for my child's father
O, how full of briers is this working-day world.

Celia. They are but burs, cousin, thrown upon thee
in holiday foolery. If we walk not in the trodden
paths, our very petticoats will catch them.　　　　　1

Rosalind. I could shake them off my coat. These
burs are in my heart.

Celia. Hem them away.

Rosalind. I would try, if I could cry 'hem' and
have him.　　　　　　　　　　　　　　　　　　　　2

Celia. Come, come, wrastle with thy affections.

Rosalind. O, they take the part of a better wrastler
than myself.

Celia. O, a good wish upon you! You will try in
time, in despite of a fall. But, turning these jests
out of service, let us talk in good earnest. Is it possible on such a sudden you should fall into so strong
a liking with old Sir Rowland's youngest son?

Rosalind. The Duke my father lov'd his father
dearly.　　　　　　　　　　　　　　　　　　　　3

Celia. Doth it therefore ensue that you should love
his son dearly? By this kind of chase I should hate
him, for my father hated his father dearly. Yet I
hate not Orlando.　　　　　　　　　　　　　　　3

Rosalind. No, faith. Hate him not, for my sake.

Celia. Why should I not? Doth he not deserve well?

Enter Duke with Lords.

Rosalind. Let me love him for that, and you do
love him because I do. Look, here comes the Duke.

18 Hem clear away with a cough. 19 'hem' . . . him N. 21 affections feelings. 25 in despite of notwithstanding. turning . . .
service putting aside. 32 chase pursuit of an argument. 36 deserve
well N.

Celia. With his eyes full of anger.   39

Duke. Mistress, dispatch you with your safest haste
And get you from our court.

Rosalind.   Me, uncle?

Duke.   You, cousin.
Within these ten days if that thou beest found
So near our public court as twenty miles,
Thou diest for it.

Rosalind.   I do beseech your Grace,
Let me the knowledge of my fault bear with me.   45
If with myself I hold intelligence,
Or have acquaintance with mine own desires;
If that I do not dream, or be not frantic—
As I do trust I am not—then, dear uncle,
Never so much as in a thought unborn   50
Did I offend your highness.

Duke.   Thus do all traitors.
If their purgation did consist in words,
They are as innocent as grace itself.
Let it suffice thee that I trust thee not.

Rosalind. Yet your mistrust cannot make me a
          traitor.   55
Tell me whereon the likelihood depends.

Duke. Thou art thy father's daughter; there's
          enough.

Rosalind. So was I when your highness took his
          dukedom;
So was I when your highness banish'd him.
Treason is not inherited, my lord;   60
Or if we did derive it from our friends,
What's that to me? My father was no traitor.

40 **dispatch you** remove yourself. 46 **hold intelligence** communi-
cate. 48 **If that** if. 52 **purgation** absolution from guilt. 53 **grace**
virtue. 56 **likelihood** possibility. 61 **friends** relatives.

Then, good my liege, mistake me not so much
To think my poverty is treacherous.
  Celia. Dear sovereign, hear me speak. 6
  Duke. Ay, Celia, we stay'd her for your sake,
Else had she with her father rang'd along.
  Celia. I did not then entreat to have her stay;
It was your pleasure, and your own remorse.
I was too young that time to value her, 70
But now I know her. If she be a traitor,
Why so am I. We still have slept together,
Rose at an instant, learn'd, play'd, eat together,
And wheresoe'er we went, like Juno's swans,
Still we went coupled and inseparable. 7
  Duke. She is too subtile for thee. And her smooth-
    ness,
Her very silence and her patience,
Speak to the people, and they pity her.
Thou art a fool. She robs thee of thy name,
And thou wilt show more bright and seem more vir-
    tuous 8
When she is gone. Then open not thy lips.
Firm and irrevocable is my doom
Which I have pass'd upon her: she is banish'd.
  Celia. Pronounce that sentence then on me, my
    liege.
I cannot live out of her company. 8
  Duke. You are a fool. You, niece, provide yourself
If you outstay the time, upon mine honor
And in the greatness of my word, you die.

                    Exeunt Duke, etc

64 **To** as to. 67 **rang'd** wandered. 69 **remorse** compassion. 72 **still**
always. 73 **Rose** risen. **at an instant** at the same time. **eat** eaten
(pronounced 'et'). 74 **Juno's swans** N. 76 **subtile** subtle, acute.
80 **show** appear. **virtuous** full of good qualities. 82 **doom** sentence.
88 **in . . . word** by my word as ruler.

   20

Celia. O my poor Rosalind, whether wilt thou go?
Wilt thou change fathers? I will give thee mine.   90
charge thee be not thou more griev'd than I am.
Rosalind. I have more cause.
Celia.   Thou hast not, cousin.
Prithee, be cheerful. Know'st thou not the Duke
Hath banish'd me, his daughter?
Rosalind.   That he hath not.
Celia. No? Hath not? Rosalind lacks then the love
Which teacheth thee that thou and I am one.   96
Shall we be sund'red? Shall we part, sweet girl?
No! Let my father seek another heir.
Therefore devise with me how we may fly,
Whether to go, and what to bear with us.   100
And do not seek to take your change upon you,
To bear your griefs yourself and leave me out.
For by this heaven, now at our sorrows pale,
Say what thou canst, I'll go along with thee.
Rosalind. Why, whether shall we go?   105
Celia. To seek my uncle in the Forest of Arden.
Rosalind. Alas, what danger will it be to us—
Maids as we are—to travel forth so far?
Beauty provoketh thieves sooner than gold.
Celia. I'll put myself in poor and mean attire   110
And with a kind of umber smirch my face;
The like do you. So shall we pass along
And never stir assailants.
Rosalind.   Were it not better,
Because that I am more than common tall,
That I did suit me all points like a man: 115
A gallant curtelaxe upon my thigh,
A boar spear in my hand, and—in my heart

99 **whether** whither. 101 **change** N. 110 **mean** lowly. 111 **umber**
brown pigment. 113 **stir** incite. 114 **than common** than usually.
115 **all points** in all respects. 116 **curtelaxe** broad sword.

21

Lie there what hidden woman's fear there will—
We'll have a swashing and a martial outside,
As many other mannish cowards have   1¦
That do outface it with their semblances.
  Celia. What shall I call thee when thou art a man
  Rosalind. I'll have no worse a name than Jove's ow
      page,
And therefore look you call me Ganymede.
But what will you be call'd?   1¦
  Celia. Something that hath a reference to my state
No longer Celia but Aliena.
  Rosalind. But, cousin, what if we assay'd to steal
The clownish Fool out of your father's court?
Would he not be a comfort to our travel?   1¦
  Celia. He'll go along o'er the wide world with me.
Leave me alone to woo him. Let's away
And get our jewels and our wealth together,
Devise the fittest time and safest way
To hide us from pursuit that will be made   1¦
After my flight. Now go we in content
To liberty, and not to banishment.   *Exeun*

119 **swashing** swaggering. 121 **outface it** brazen it out. **semblanc**
appearances. 124 **Ganymede** N. 127 **Aliena** the cast off (Latin
128 **assay'd** attempted. 132 **woo** persuade. 136 **in content** satisfie

22

Act II

SCENE 1

Enter Duke Senior, Amiens, and two or three Lords like Foresters.

Duke Senior. Now, my co-mates and brothers in
        exile,
Hath not old custom made this life more sweet
Than that of painted pomp? Are not these woods
More free from peril than the envious court?
Here feel we not the penalty of Adam,   5
The seasons' difference?—as, the icy fang
And churlish chiding of the winter's wind
Which when it bites and blows upon my body
E'en till I shrink with cold, I smile and say:
'This is no flattery; these are counselors   10
That feelingly persuade me what I am.'
Sweet are the uses of adversity,
Which, like the toad, ugly and venomous,
Wears yet a precious jewel in his head.
And this our life, exempt from public haunt,   15
Finds tongues in trees, books in the running brooks,
Sermons in stones, and good in everything.
Amiens. I would not change it. Happy is your grace
That can translate the stubborness of Fortune
Into so quiet and so sweet a style.   20

1 **exile** stressed — ´. 3 **painted** artificial N. 5 **the penalty of Adam** N. 6 **as** for example. 7 **churlish** rough. 9 **E'en** F *Even.* 12 **uses** benefits. 13 **toad** N. 15 **public haunt** resorts of men. 18 **Amiens** N. 20 **style** i.e. of life.

Duke Senior. Come, shall we go and kill us venison?
And yet it irks me the poor dappled fools,
Being native burghers of this desert city,
Should in their own confines with forked heads   24
Have their round hanches gor'd.

   1 Lord.   Indeed, my lord,
The melancholy Jaques grieves at that,
And in that kind swears you do more usurp
Than doth your brother that hath banish'd you.
Today my Lord of Amiens and myself
Did steal behind him as he lay along   30
Under an oak whose anticke root peeps out
Upon the brook that brawls along this wood.
To the which place a poor sequest'red stag,
That from the hunter's aim had tane a hurt,
Did come to languish. And indeed, my lord,   35
The wretched animal heav'd forth such groans
That their discharge did stretch his leathern coat
Almost to bursting, and the big round tears
Cours'd one another down his innocent nose
In piteous chase. And thus the hairy fool,   40
Much marked of the melancholy Jaques,
Stood on th' extremest verge of the swift brook,
Augmenting it with tears.

   Duke Senior.   But what said Jaques?
Did he not moralize this spectacle?

   1 Lord. O yes, into a thousand similes.   45
First, for his weeping into the needless stream:
'Poor deer,' quoth he, 'thou mak'st a testament

---

23 **desert** uninhabited. 24 **confines** territory. **forked heads** hunting arrows. 25 **hanches** haunches. 26 **Jaques** N. 27 **in that kind** in that respect. 30 **along** stretched out. 31 **anticke** old (stressed
$\acute{-}$ —). 32 **brawls** courses. 33 **sequest'red** separated from the herd. 41 **of** by. 42 **verge** bank. 44 **moralize** make a sermon on. 46 **needless** i.e. not needing any more water.

24

As worldlings do, giving thy sum of more
To that which had too much.' Then, being there
    alone,
Left and abandoned of his velvet friends: 50
' 'Tis right,' quoth he, 'thus misery doth part
The flux of company.' Anon a careless herd,
Full of the pasture, jumps along by him
And never stays to greet him. 'Ay,' quoth Jaques,
'Sweep on, you fat and greasy citizens;   55
'Tis just the fashion. Wherefore do you look
Upon that poor and broken bankrupt there?'
Thus most invectively he pierceth through
The body of the country, city, court,
Yea, and of this our life, swearing that we   60
Are mere usurpers, tyrants, and what's worse,
To fright the animals and to kill them up
In their assign'd and native dwelling place.
   Duke Senior. And did you leave him in this con-
    templation?   64
   2 Lord. We did, my Lord, weeping and commenting
Upon the sobbing deer.
   Duke Senior.   Show me the place.
I love to cope him in these sullen fits,
For then he's full of matter.
   1 Lord. I'll bring you to him straight.   *Exeunt.*

48 **worldlings** people of the world. 49 **there** N. 50 **of** by. **velvet** N.
51 **part** part from. 52 **flux** stream. **Anon** presently. 58 **invectively**
with denunciation. 59 **the** (before *country*) F omits. 62 **kill . . . up**
kill off. 67 **cope** meet. 68 **matter** substance. 69 **straight** immediately.

SCENE 2

Enter Duke [Frederick], with Lords.

Duke. Can it be possible that no man saw them?
It cannot be; some villains of my court
Are of consent and sufferance in this.
  1 Lord. I cannot hear of any that did see her.
The ladies, her attendants of her chamber,   5
Saw her abed, and in the morning early
They found the bed untreasur'd of their mistress.
  2 Lord. My lord, the roynish Clown at whom so oft
Your Grace was wont to laugh is also missing.
Hisperia, the princess' gentlewoman,   10
Confesses that she secretly o'erheard
Your daughter and her cousin much commend
The parts and graces of the wrastler
That did but lately foil the sinewy Charles.
And she believes, wherever they are gone,   15
That youth is surely in their company.
  Duke. Send to his brother; fetch that gallant
    hither.
If he be absent, bring his brother to me.
I'll make him find him. Do this suddenly,
And let not search and inquisition quail   20
To bring again these foolish runaways.   *Exeunt.*

3 **Are . . . sufferance** have agreed and contrived. 8 **roynish**
mangy. 13 **wrastler** here three syllables, 'wrasteler.' 19 **suddenly**
immediately. 20 **inquisition** investigation. **quail** falter.

26

SCENE 3

Enter Orlando and Adam.

Orlando. Who's there?

Adam. What, my young master! O my gentle master,
O my sweet master, O you memory
Of old Sir Rowland. Why, what make you here?   4
Why are you virtuous? Why do people love you?
And wherefore are you gentle, strong, and valiant?
Why would you be so fond to overcome
The bonny prizer of the humorous Duke?
Your praise is come too swiftly home before you.
Know you not, master, to some kind of men   10
Their graces serve them but as enemies?
No more do yours: your virtues, gentle master,
Are sanctified and holy traitors to you.
O what a world is this, when what is comely
Envenoms him that bears it.   15

Orlando. Why, what's the matter?

Adam.   O unhappy
       youth,
Come not within these doors. Within this roof
The enemy of all your graces lives.
Your brother—no, no brother, yet the son
(Yet not the son, I will not call him son)   20
Of him I was about to call his father—
Hath heard your praises and this night he means

SD **Enter . . . Adam** N. 3 **memory** reminder. 4 **make you** are
you doing. 5 **virtuous** full of good qualities. 7 **fond** foolish. 8 **bonny
prizer** sturdy prize fighter. 15 **envenoms** poisons. 18 **graces** virtues.

To burn the lodging where you use to lie,
And you within it. If he fail of that,
He will have other means to cut you off.   25
I overheard him and his practices.
This is no place: this house is but a butchery.
Abhor it, fear it, do not enter it.
   Orlando. Why, whether, Adam, would'st thou have
    me go?   29
   Adam. No matter whether, so you come not here.
   Orlando. What, would'st thou have me go and beg
    my food?
Or with a base and boist'rous sword enforce
A thievish living on the common road?
This I must do, or know not what to do;
Yet this I will not do, do how I can.   35
I rather will subject me to the malice
Of a diverted blood and bloody brother.
   Adam. But do not so. I have five hundred crowns,
The thrifty hire I saved under your father,
Which I did store to be my foster nurse   40
When service should in my old limbs lie lame
And unregarded age in corners thrown.
Take that; and He that doth the ravens feed,
Yea, providently caters for the sparrow,
Be comfort to my age. Here is the gold;   45
All this I give you. Let me be your servant.
Though I look old, yet I am strong and lusty;
For in my youth I never did apply
Hot and rebellious liquors in my blood,
Nor did not with unbashful forehead woo   50
The means of weakness and debility.

---

23 **use** are accustomed. 26 **practices** plots. 27 **place** i.e. for Orlando. **butchery** slaughterhouse. 29 **whether** whither. 32 **boist'rous**
violent. 37 **diverted blood** unnatural relationship. 39 **thrifty hire**
wages economically saved.

Therefore my age is as a lusty winter,
Frosty but kindly. Let me go with you;
I'll do the service of a younger man
In all your business and necessities.   55
  Orlando. O good old man, how well in thee appears
The constant service of the antique world,
When service sweat for duty, not for meed.
Thou art not for the fashion of these times,
Where none will sweat but for promotion,   60
And having that, do choke their service up
Even with the having; it is not so with thee.
But, poor old man, thou prun'st a rotten tree
That cannot so much as a blossom yield,
In lieu of all thy pains and husbandry.   65
But come thy ways; we'll go along together,
And ere we have thy youthful wages spent,
We'll light upon some settled low content.
  Adam. Master, go on and I will follow thee
To the last gasp with truth and loyalty.   70
From seventeen years till now almost fourscore
Here lived I; but now live here no more.
At seventeen years many their fortunes seek,
But at fourscore it is too late a week.
Yet Fortune cannot recompense me better   75
Than to die well, and not my master's debtor.
                                                    Exeunt.

57 **constant** faithful. **antique** ancient (stressed $\acute{-}$ —). 58 **sweat**
sweated. **meed** reward. 65 **In lieu of** in return for. 66 **come thy
ways** come along. 68 **low** lowly. **content** peace. 74 **too late a week**
far too late.

29

SCENE 4

*Enter Rosalind for Ganymede, Celia for Aliena, and
Clown, alias Touchstone.*

Rosalind. O Jupiter, how weary are my spirits!

Touchstone. I care not for my spirits, if my legs
were not weary.

Rosalind. I could find in my heart to disgrace my
man's apparel and to cry like a woman. But I must
comfort the weaker vessel, as doublet and hose ought
to show itself courageous to petticoat. Therefore
courage, good Aliena.

Celia. I pray you, bear with me. I cannot go no
further.   10

Touchstone. For my part, I had rather bear with
you than bear you. Yet I should bear no cross if
I did bear you, for I think you have no money in your
purse.

Rosalind. Well, this is the Forest of Arden.   15

Touchstone. Ay, now am I in Arden, the more fool
I. When I was at home I was in a better place, but
travelers must be content.

Enter Corin and Silvius.

Rosalind. Ay, be so, good Touchstone. Look you,
who comes here—a young man and an old in solemn
talk.   21

Corin. That is the way to make her scorn you still.

Silvius. O Corin, that thou knew'st how I do love
   her.

Corin. I partly guess, for I have lov'd ere now.

1 weary N. 6 weaker vessel woman. doublet and hose Elizabethan male costume of jacket and tights. 12 cross N. 16 Arden
N.

Silvius. No, Corin. Being old, thou canst not guess,
Though in thy youth thou wast as true a lover   26
As ever sigh'd upon a midnight pillow.
But if thy love were ever like to mine—
As sure I think did never man love so—
How many actions most ridiculous   30
Hast thou been drawn to by thy fantasy?
  Corin. Into a thousand that I have forgotten.
  Silvius. O thou didst then ne'er love so heartily.
If thou rememb'rest not the slightest folly
That ever love did make thee run into,   35
Thou hast not lov'd.
Or if thou hast not sat as I do now,
Wearing thy hearer in thy mistress' praise,
Thou hast not lov'd.
Or if thou hast not broke from company   40
Abruptly as my passion now makes me,
Thou hast not lov'd.
O Phebe, Phebe, Phebe!   *Exit.*
  Rosalind. Alas, poor shepherd! Searching of thy
          wound,
I have by hard adventure found mine own.
  Touchstone. And I mine. I remember when I was in
love, I broke my sword upon a stone and bid him
take that for coming a-night to Jane Smile. And I
remember the kissing of her batler and the cow's
dugs that her pretty chopt hands had milk'd. And
I remember the wooing of a peascod instead of her,
from whom I took two cods, and giving them her
again, said with weeping tears: 'Wear these for my
sake.' We that are true lovers run into strange

31 fantasy love. 33 ne'er F *never.* 38 Wearing wearying.
44 Searching of probing. 45 hard adventure misfortune. 48
a-night at night. 49 batler a stick for beating clothes. 50 chopt
chapped. 51 peascod peapod.

31

capers. But as all is mortal in nature, so is all nature in love mortal in folly.   56

Rosalind. Thou speak'st wiser than thou art ware
of.

Touchstone. Nay, I shall ne'er be ware of mine own
wit till I break my shins against it.   60

Rosalind. Jove, Jove, this shepherd's passion
Is much upon my fashion.

Touchstone. And mine. But it grows something stale
    with me.

Celia. I pray you, one of you question yond man,
If he for gold will give us any food.   65
I faint almost to death.

Touchstone.   Holla, you clown!

Rosalind. Peace, fool! He's not thy kinsman.

Corin.   Who
    calls?

Touchstone. Your betters, sir.

Corin.   Else are they very
    wretched.

Rosalind. Peace, I say! Good even to you, friend.

Corin. And to you, gentle sir, and to you all.   70

Rosalind. I prithee, shepherd, if that love or gold
Can in this desert place buy entertainment,
Bring us where we may rest ourselves and feed.
Here's a young maid with travel much oppress'd,
And faints for succor.

Corin.   Fair sir, I pity her,   75
And wish for her sake more than for mine own
My fortunes were more able to relieve her.
But I am shepherd to another man,

55 **capers** pranks. **mortal** N. 57 **ware** aware. 63 **something** somewhat. 64 **yond** yonder. 66 **clown** peasant. 67 **kinsman** N. 72 **entertainment** hospitality. 75 **succor** aid.

32

And do not shear the fleeces that I graze.
My master is of churlish disposition,   80
And little recks to find the way to heaven
By doing deeds of hospitality.
Besides, his cote, his flocks, and bounds of feed
Are now on sale; and at our sheepcote now,
By reason of his absence, there is nothing   85
That you will feed on. But what is, come see,
And in my voice most welcome shall you be.
   Rosalind. What is he that shall buy his flock and
     pasture?
   Corin. That young swain that you saw here but
     erewhile,
That little cares for buying anything.   90
   Rosalind. I pray thee, if it stand with honesty,
Buy thou the cottage, pasture, and the flock,
And thou shalt have to pay for it of us.
   Celia. And we will mend thy wages. I like this place
And willingly could waste my time in it.   95
   Corin. Assuredly the thing is to be sold.
Go with me. If you like, upon report,
The soil, the profit, and this kind of life,
I will your very faithful feeder be   99
And buy it with your gold right suddenly.   *Exeunt.*

80 **churlish** niggardly. 81 **recks** cares. 83 **cote** cottage. **bounds of feed** extent of pasturage. 87 **in my voice** for my part. 88 **What** who. 89 **but erewhile** just now. 91 **stand** be consistent. 93 **have to pay** have money to pay. 94 **mend** raise. 95 **waste** pass. 99 **feeder** servant.

SCENE 5

Enter Amiens, Jaques, and others.

Song

[*Amiens.*] Under the greenwood tree
Who loves to lie with me,
And turn his merry note
Unto the sweet bird's throat,
Come hither, come hither, come hither! 5
Here shall he see
No enemy
But winter and rough weather.

Jaques. More, more, I prithee, more. 9

Amiens. It will make you melancholy, Monsieur Jaques.

Jaques. I thank it. More, I prithee, more. I can suck melancholy out of a song as a weasel sucks eggs. More, I prithee, more. 14

Amiens. My voice is ragged; I know I cannot please you.

Jaques. I do not desire you to please me; I do desire you to sing. Come, more: another stanzo. Call you 'em stanzos?

Amiens. What you will, Monsieur Jaques. 20

Jaques. Nay, I care not for their names; they owe me nothing. Will you sing?

Amiens. More at your request than to please myself. 24

Jaques. Well then, if ever I thank any man, I'll thank you. But that they call compliment is like

3 turn adapt. 15 ragged uneven. 18 stanzo stanza. 21 names i.e. signatures on a bond of debt. 26 that what. compliment courtesy.

34

th' encounter of two dog-apes. And when a man thanks me heartily, methinks I have given him a penny, and he renders me the beggarly thanks. Come, sing. And you that will not, hold your tongues.

Amiens. Well, I'll end the song. Sirs, cover the while; the Duke will drink under this tree. He hath been all this day to look you.

Jaques. And I have been all this day to avoid him. He is too disputable for my company. I think of as many matters as he, but I give heaven thanks and make no boast of them. Come, warble, come.

Song

All together here.

> Who doth ambition shun
> And loves to lie i' th' sun,
> Seeking the food he eats   40
> And pleas'd with what he gets,
> Come hither, come hither, come hither!
> Here shall he see
> No enemy
> But winter and rough weather.   45

Jaques. I'll give you a verse to this note that I made yesterday in despite of my invention.

Amiens. And I'll sing it.

Jaques. Thus it goes:

> If it do come to pass   50
> That any man turn ass,
> Leaving his wealth and ease,
> A stubborn will to please,
> Ducdame, ducdame, ducdame!

27 **dog-apes** dog-faced baboons. 31 **cover the while** set the table now. 33 **look** look for. 35 **disputable** prone to argue. 46 **note** tune. 47 **in . . . invention** without using my imagination. 54 **Ducdame** N.

35

Here shall he see   55
Gross fools as he,
And if he will come to me.

Amiens. What's that 'ducdame'?

Jaques. 'Tis a Greek invocation to call fools into a circle. I'll go sleep if I can; if I cannot, I'll rail against all the first born of Egypt.   61

Amiens. And I'll go seek the Duke. His banket is prepar'd.   *Exeunt.*

SCENE 6

Enter Orlando and Adam.

Adam. Dear master, I can go no further. O, I die for food! Here lie I down and measure out my grave. Farewell, kind master.

Orlando. Why, how now, Adam? No greater heart in thee? Live a little, comfort a little, cheer thyself a little. If this uncouth forest yield anything savage, I will either be food for it or bring it for food to thee. Thy conceit is nearer death than thy powers. For my sake, be comfortable; hold death awhile at the arm's end. I will here be with thee presently, and if I bring thee not something to eat, I will give thee leave to die; but if thou diest before I come, thou art a mocker of my labor. Well said. Thou look'st cheerly, and I'll be with thee quickly. Yet thou liest in the bleak air. Come, I will bear thee to some shelter, and thou shalt not die for lack of a dinner, if

57 **And if** an if, if only. 60 **circle** N. 61 **first born of Egypt** N. 62 **banket** banquet, a light meal of fruit and wine. 5 **comfort a little** take comfort. 6 **uncouth** unknown. 8 **conceit** imagination. 10 **presently** immediately. 13 **Well said** well done. 14 **cheerly** cheerful.

there live anything in this desert. Cheerly, good
Adam.   *Exeunt.*

SCENE 7

*Enter Duke Senior, [Amiens,] and Lord, like
Outlaws.*

Duke Senior. I think he be transform'd into a beast,
For I can nowhere find him like a man.
1 Lord. My lord, he is but even now gone hence.
Here was he merry, hearing of a song.   4
Duke Senior. If he, compact of jars, grow musical,
We shall have shortly discord in the spheres.
Go seek him; tell him I would speak with him.

Enter Jaques.

1 Lord. He saves my labor by his own approach.
Duke Senior. Why, how now, monsieur! What a life
    is this   9
That your poor friends must woo your company.
What, you look merrily.
Jaques. A fool, a fool. I met a fool i' th' forest,
A motley fool—a miserable world.
As I do live by food I met a fool,
Who laid him down and bask'd him in the sun,   15
And rail'd on Lady Fortune in good terms,
In good set terms; and yet a motley fool.
'Good morrow, fool,' quoth I. 'No, sir,' quoth he,
'Call me not fool till heaven hath sent me fortune.'
And then he drew a dial from his poke,   20

1 **be is** (the subjunctive form). 5 **compact of jars** made up of
discord. 6 **discord . . . spheres** N. 11 **merrily** cheerful. 13 **motley**
N. 17 **good set terms** precise terms. 20 **dial** sundial. **poke**
pocket.

37

And looking on it with lackluster eye,
Says, very wisely: 'It is ten o'clock.'
'Thus we may see,' quoth he, 'how the world wags.
'Tis but an hour ago since it was nine,
And after one hour more 'twill be eleven.   25
And so from hour to hour we ripe and ripe,
And then from hour to hour we rot and rot.
And thereby hangs a tale.' When I did hear
The motley fool thus moral on the time,
My lungs began to crow like Chanticleer   30
That fools should be so deep contemplative.
And I did laugh sans intermission,
An hour by his dial. O noble fool,
A worthy fool! Motley's the only wear.
    Duke Senior. What fool is this?   35
    Jaques. O worthy fool—one that hath been a cour-
        tier
And says, if ladies be but young and fair,
They have the gift to know it. And in his brain,
Which is as dry as the remainder biscuit   39
After a voyage, he hath strange places cramm'd
With observation, the which he vents
In mangled forms. O that I were a fool!
I am ambitious for a motley coat.
    Duke Senior. Thou shalt have one.
    Jaques.   It is my only
        suit.
Provided that you weed your better judgments   45
Of all opinion that grows rank in them,
That I am wise. I must have liberty

23 wags moves along. 26 **hour** N. ripe grow ripe N. 29 **moral**
moralize. 30 **Chanticleer** N. 31 **deep** deeply. 32 **sans** without.
39 **remainder biscuit** stale hardtack. 41 **vents** utters. 44 **suit** N.
46 **rank** luxuriant.

38

Withal, as large a charter as the wind
To blow on whom I please, for so fools have.
And they that are most galled with my folly,   50
They most must laugh. And why, sir, must they so?
The 'why' is plain as way to parish church:
He that a fool doth very wisely hit
Doth very foolishly, although he smart,
Not to seem senseless of the bob. If not,   55
The wise man's folly is anatomiz'd
E'en by the squand'ring glances of the fool.
Invest me in my motley. Give me leave
To speak my mind, and I will through and through
Cleanse the foul body of th' infected world,   60
If they will patiently receive my medicine.
Duke Senior. Fie on thee. I can tell what thou
    would'st do.
Jaques. What, for a counter, would I do but good?
Duke Senior. Most mischievous foul sin in chiding
    sin;
For thou thyself hath been a libertine   65
As sensual as the brutish sting itself.
And all th' embossed sores and headed evils
That thou with license of free foot hast caught,
Would'st thou disgorge into the general world.
Jaques. Why, who cries out on pride   70
That can therein tax any private party?
Doth it not flow as hugely as the sea,
Till that the weary very means do ebb?

48 **Withal** too. **charter** license. 50 **galled** irritated. 54 **Doth very
foolishly** acts very foolishly. 55 **Not to** F omits. **senseless** insen-
sible. **bob** taunt. 56 **anatomiz'd** analyzed. 57 **E'en** F *Even.* **squan-
d'ring** random. 58 **Invest** clothe. 63 **counter** coin of little value,
i.e. a wager. 66 **sting** lust. 67 **embossed** swollen. 69 **general** whole
(to be read 'gen'ral'). 71 **tax** criticize. 73 **weary very means** N.

What woman in the city do I name,
When that I say the city woman bears   75
The cost of princes on unworthy shoulders?
Who can come in and say that I mean her,
When such a one as thee, such is her neighbor?
Or what is he of basest function
That says his bravery is not on my cost,   80
Thinking that I mean him, but therein suits
His folly to the mettle of my speech?
There then. How then? What then? Let me see
          wherein
My tongue hath wrong'd him. If it do him right,
Then he hath wrong'd himself; if he be free,   85
Why then my taxing, like a wild goose, flies
Unclaim'd of any man. But who comes here?

Enter Orlando [with sword drawn].

Orlando. Forbear, and eat no more.
Jaques.   Why, I have
          eat none yet.
Orlando. Nor shalt not, till necessity be serv'd.   89
Jaques. Of what kind should this cock come of?
Duke Senior. Art thou thus bolden'd, man, by thy
          distress,
Or else a rude despiser of good manners,
That in civility thou seem'st so empty?
Orlando. You touch'd my vein at first. The thorny
          point
Of bare distress hath tane from me the show   95
Of smooth civility; yet am I inland bred

80 **bravery** elaborate dress (to be read 'brav'ry'). **on my cost** at
my expense. 82 **mettle** substance. 85 **free** not guilty. 88 **Forbear**
abstain. 91 **bolden'd** emboldened. 93 **civility** courtesy. 94 **touch'd
my vein** hit my feelings. 96 **inland bred** civilized.
          40

And know some nurture. But forbear, I say.
He dies that touches any of this fruit
Till I and my affairs are answered.   99
  Jaques. And you will not be answer'd with reason,
I must die.
  Duke Senior. What would you have? Your gentle-
    ness shall force
More than your force move us to gentleness.
  Orlando. I almost die for food, and let me have it.
  Duke Senior. Sit down and feed, and welcome to
    our table.   105
  Orlando. Speak you so gently? Pardon me, I pray
    you.
I thought that all things had been savage here,
And therefore put I on the countenance
Of stern commandment. But—whate'er you are
That in this desert inaccessible   110
Under the shade of melancholy boughs
Lose and neglect the creeping hours of time—
If ever you have look'd on better days,
If ever been where bells have knoll'd to church,
If ever sat at any good man's feast,   115
If ever from your eyelids wip'd a tear
And know what 'tis to pity and be pitied,
Let gentleness my strong enforcement be.
In the which hope I blush and hide my sword.
  Duke Senior. True it is that we have seen better
    days,   120
And have with holy bell been knoll'd to church,
And sat at good men's feasts, and wip'd our eyes
Of drops that sacred pity hath engend'red.

97 **nurture** good breeding. 99 **answered** provided for. 100 **And**
an (if). **reason** N. 109 **commandment** authority. 114 **knoll'd**
tolled. 118 **enforcement** support.

And therefore sit you down in gentleness,
And take upon command what help we have   125
That to your wanting may be minist'red.
  Orlando. Then but forbear your food a little while,
Whiles like a doe I go to find my fawn
And give it food. There is an old poor man,
Who after me hath many a weary step   130
Limp'd in pure love. Till he be first suffic'd,
Oppress'd with two weak evils, age and hunger,
I will not touch a bit.
  Duke Senior.   Go find him out,
And we will nothing waste till you return.
  Orlando. I thank ye, and be blest for your good
      comfort.   *Exit.*
  Duke Senior. Thou seest we are not all alone un-
      happy.   136
This wide and universal theater
Presents more woeful pageants than the scene
Wherein we play in.
  Jaques.   All the world's a stage,
And all the men and women merely players.   140
They have their exits and their entrances,
And one man in his time plays many parts,
His acts being seven ages. At first the infant,
Mewling and puking in the nurse's arms.
Then the whining schoolboy with his satchel   145
And shining morning face, creeping like snail
Unwillingly to school. And then the lover,
Sighing like furnace, with a woeful ballad
Made to his mistress' eyebrow. Then a soldier,
Full of strange oaths and bearded like the pard,   150

125 **upon command** at your pleasure. 126 **wanting** need. 132 **weak** causing weakness. 135 **comfort** help. 144 **Mewling** crying, mewing like a cat. 150 **pard** leopard.

42

Jealous in honor, sudden and quick in quarrel,
Seeking the bubble Reputation
E'en in the cannon's mouth. And then the justice,
In fair round belly with good capon lin'd,
With eyes severe and beard of formal cut,   155
Full of wise saws and modern instances;
And so he plays his part. The sixt age shifts
Into the lean and slipper'd pantaloon,
With spectacles on nose and pouch on side;
His youthful hose well sav'd, a world too wide   160
For his shrunk shank, and his big manly voice,
Turning again toward childish treble, pipes
And whistles in his sound. Last scene of all,
That ends this strange eventful history,
Is second childishness and mere oblivion—   165
Sans teeth, sans eyes, sans taste, sans everything.

Enter Orlando with Adam.

Duke Senior. Welcome. Set down your venerable
    burthen,
And let him feed.
    Orlando. I thank you most for him.
    Adam.   So had you
    need;
I scarce can speak to thank you for myself.   170
    Duke Senior. Welcome; fall to. I will not trouble
    you
As yet to question you about your fortunes.
Give us some music and, good cousin, sing.

151 **Jealous in** suspiciously careful of. 153 **E'en** F *Even.* 156 **saws** maxims. **modern instances** everyday illustrations. 157 **sixt** sixth. 158 **pantaloon** old dotard N. 163 **his** its. 165 **mere** total. 166 **Sans** without. 167 **burthen** burden.

Song

[*Amiens.*] Blow, blow, thou winter wind
        Thou art not so unkind   175
           As man's ingratitude.
        Thy tooth is not so keen
        Because thou art not seen,
           Although thy breath be rude.
  Heigh ho, sing heigh ho, unto the green holly!   180
  Most friendship is feigning, most loving mere folly:
        Then heigh ho, the holly,
        This life is most jolly.

        Freeze, freeze, thou bitter sky,
        That dost not bite so nigh   185
           As benefits forgot.
        Though thou the waters warp,
        Thy sting is not so sharp
           As friend rememb'red not.
  Heigh ho, sing, etc.   190

Duke Senior. If that you were the good Sir Row-
    land's son,
As you have whisper'd faithfully you were,
And as mine eye doth his effigies witness
Most truly limn'd and living in your face,
Be truly welcome hither. I am the Duke   195
That lov'd your father. The residue of your fortune,
Go to my cave and tell me. Good old man,
Thou art right welcome, as thy master is.
Support him by the arm. Give me your hand,   199
And let me all your fortunes understand.   *Exeunt.*

187 warp i.e. by turning into ice. 193 **effigies** likeness (stressed
— ́ —). 194 **limn'd** portrayed.

Act III

SCENE 1

Enter Duke [Frederick], Lords, and Oliver.

Duke. Not see him since? Sir, sir, that cannot be.
But were I not the better part made mercy,
I should not seek an absent argument
Of my revenge, thou present. But look to it:
Find out thy brother, wheresoe'er he is;   5
Seek him with candle; bring him dead or living
Within this twelvemonth, or turn thou no more
To seek a living in our territory.
Thy lands and all things that thou dost call thine,
Worth seizure, do we seize into our hands,   10
Till thou canst quit thee by thy brother's mouth
Of what we think against thee.
  Oliver. O that your highness knew my heart in this.
I never lov'd my brother in my life.
  Duke. More villain thou. Well, push him out of
    doors,   15
And let my officers of such a nature
Make an extent upon his house and lands.
Do this expediently, and turn him going.   *Exeunt.*

2 made mercy made of mercy. 3 argument object, i.e. Orlando.
6 candle N. 7 turn return. 11 quit absolve. 16 of such a nature
whose business it is. 17 extent seizure. 18 expediently expedi-
tiously.

SCENE 2

Enter Orlando.

Orlando. Hang there, my verse, in witness of my
  love.
And thou, thrice crowned Queen of Night, survey
With thy chaste eye, from thy pale sphere above,
Thy huntress' name that my full life doth sway.
O Rosalind, these trees shall be my books   5
And in their barks my thoughts I'll character,
That every eye which in this forest looks
Shall see thy virtue witness'd everywhere.
Run, run, Orlando! Carve on every tree
The fair, the chaste, and unexpressive she. *Exit.* 10

Enter Corin and Clown [Touchstone].

Corin. And how like you this shepherd's life, Master
Touchstone?

Touchstone. Truly, shepherd, in respect of itself it
is a good life; but in respect that it is a shepherd's
life, it is naught. In respect that it is solitary, I like
it very well; but in respect that it is private, it is a
very vild life. Now, in respect it is in the fields, it
pleaseth me well; but in respect it is not in the
court, it is tedious. As it is a spare life, look you, it
fits my humor well; but as there is no more plenty in
it, it goes much against my stomach. Hast any philosophy in thee, shepherd?   22

Corin. No more but that I know the more one sick-

2 Queen of Night the moon N. 4 huntress' name N. full entire.
sway rule. 6 character inscribe. 7 That so that. 10 unexpressive
indescribable. 15 naught worthless. 16 private lonely. 17 vild
vile. 19 spare frugal. 21 philosophy science, general knowledge.

ens, the worse at ease he is; and that he that wants
money, means, and content is without three good
friends; that the property of rain is to wet, and
fire to burn; that good pasture makes fat sheep; and
that a great cause of the night is lack of the sun;
that he that hath learned no wit by nature nor art
may complain of good breeding, or comes of a very
dull kindred.   31

Touchstone. Such a one is a natural philosopher.
Wast ever in court, shepherd?

Corin. No, truly.

Touchstone. Then thou art damn'd.   35

Corin. Nay, I hope.

Touchstone. Truly thou art damn'd like an ill-
roasted egg, all on one side.

Corin. For not being at court? Your reason.   39

Touchstone. Why, if thou never wast at court, thou
never saw'st good manners. If thou never saw'st
good manners, then thy manners must be wicked;
and wickedness is sin, and sin is damnation. Thou
art in a parlous state, shepherd.   44

Corin. Not a whit, Touchstone. Those that are
good manners at the court are as ridiculous in the
country as the behavior of the country is most
mockable at the court. You told me you salute not at
the court, but you kiss your hands. That courtesy
would be uncleanly if courtiers were shepherds.   50

Touchstone. Instance briefly. Come, instance.

Corin. Why, we are still handling our ewes, and
their fells you know are greasy.

Touchstone. Why, do not your courtier's hands

29 wit knowledge. 30 **complain . . . breeding** complain of the
lack of good breeding. 41 **manners** N. 49 **but** unless. 51 **Instance**
give an example. 52 **still** always. 53 **fells** fleeces.

sweat? And is not the grease of a mutton as whole-
some as the sweat of a man? Shallow, shallow. A
better instance, I say. Come.

Corin. Besides, our hands are hard.

Touchstone. Your lips will feel them the sooner.
Shallow again. A more sounder instance, come.   60

Corin. And they are often tarr'd over with the
surgery of our sheep. And would you have us kiss
tar? The courtier's hands are perfum'd with civet.

Touchstone. Most shallow man, thou worm's meat
in respect of a good piece of flesh indeed, learn of the
wise and perpend: civet is of baser birth than tar,
the very uncleanly flux of a cat. Mend the instance,
shepherd.

Corin. You have too courtly a wit for me. I'll rest.

Touchstone. Wilt thou rest damn'd? God help thee,
shallow man. God make incision in thee; thou art
raw.   72

Corin. Sir, I am a true laborer. I earn that I eat,
get that I wear; owe no man hate, envy no man's
happiness; glad of other men's good, content with
my harm; and the greatest of my pride is to see my
ewes graze and my lambs suck.   77

Touchstone. That is another simple sin in you—to
bring the ewes and the rams together and to offer
to get your living by the copulation of cattle; to be
bawd to a bellwether and to betray a she-lamb of a
twelvemonth to a crooked-pated old cuckoldly ram,

61 **tarr'd** N. 63 **civet** perfume derived from the civet cat. 64
worm's meat food for worms. 65 **in respect of** in comparison with.
66 **perpend** consider. 67 **flux** discharge. **Mend** improve. 71 **incision**
an operation (to cure his folly). 72 **raw** inexperienced, simple
(with a pun on 'sore'). 73 **that** what. 78 **simple** foolish. 79 **offer**
undertake. 81 **bellwether** the leading sheep in a flock carries a
bell. 82 **cuckoldly** N.

out of all reasonable match. If thou beest not damn'd
for this, the divell himself will have no shepherds. I
cannot see else how thou shouldst scape. 85

Corin. Here comes young Master Ganymede, my
new mistress' brother.

Enter Rosalind [*reading from a paper*].

Rosalind. From the east to western Ind,
  No jewel is like Rosalind.
  Her worth being mounted on the wind, 90
  Through all the world bears Rosalind.
  All the pictures fairest lin'd
  Are but black to Rosalind.
  Let no face be kept in mind
  But the fair of Rosalind. 95

Touchstone. I'll rhyme you so eight years together,
dinners and suppers and sleeping hours excepted.
It is the right butter-women's rank to market.

Rosalind. Out, fool!

Touchstone. For a taste: 100

  If a hart do lack a hind,
  Let him seek out Rosalind.
  If the cat will after kind,
  So be sure will Rosalind.
  Winter garments must be lin'd; 105
  So must slender Rosalind.
  They that reap must sheaf and bind,
  Then to cart with Rosalind.
  Sweetest nut hath sourest rind:
  Such a nut is Rosalind. 110
  He that sweetest rose will find,
  Must find love's prick and Rosalind.

83 **out . . . match** a quite unsuitable match. 84 **divell** devil.
88 **Ind** N. 92 **lin'd** drawn. 95 **fair** i.e. fair face. 98 **right** precise.
butter-women's rank N. 99 **Out** away with you. 100 **taste** sample.
103 **after kind** follow nature. 108 **to cart** N.

This is the very false gallop of verses. Why do you infect yourself with them?   114

Rosalind. Peace, you dull fool. I found them on a tree.

Touchstone. Truly the tree yields bad fruit.

Rosalind. I'll graff it with you, and then I shall graff it with a medlar. Then it will be the earliest fruit i' th' country: for you'll be rotten ere you be half ripe, and that's the right virtue of the medlar.

Touchstone. You have said; but whether wisely or no, let the forest judge.   124

Enter Celia with a writing.

Rosalind. Peace! Here comes my sister reading; stand aside.

Celia. Why should this a desert be?
   For it is unpeopled? No.
  Tongues I'll hang on every tree
   That shall civil sayings show: 130
  Some, how brief the life of man
   Runs his erring pilgrimage,
  That the stretching of a span
   Buckles in his sum of age;
  Some, of violated vows   135
   'Twixt the souls of friend and friend.
  But upon the fairest boughs,
   Or at every sentence end,
  Will I 'Rosalinda' write,
   Teaching all that read to know   140
  The quintessence of every sprite
   Heaven would in little show.

118 graff graft. you a pun on 'yew.' 119 medlar N. 121 right virtue proper characteristic. 127 a F omits. 128 For because. 130 civil polite. 132 erring wandering. 134 Buckles in limits. 141 quintessence the most highly refined essence (stressed $\acute{-} - \acute{-}$). 142 in little in miniature.

> Therefore heaven nature charg'd
>   That one body should be fill'd
> With all graces wide enlarg'd.   145
>   Nature presently distill'd
> Helen's cheek but not her heart,
>   Cleopatra's majesty,
> Atalanta's better part,
>   Sad Lucretia's modesty.   150
> Thus Rosalind of many parts
>   By heavenly synod was devis'd,
> Of many faces, eyes, and hearts,
>   To have the touches dearest priz'd.
> Heaven would that she these gifts should have,   155
>   And I to live and die her slave.

Rosalind. O most gentle Jupiter, what tedious homily of love have you wearied your parishioners withal and never cried: 'Have patience, good people.'

Celia. How now? Back, friends. Shepherd, go off a little; go with him, sirrah.   161

Touchstone. Come, shepherd. Let us make an honorable retreat, though not with bag and baggage, yet with scrip and scrippage.   *Exeunt.*

Celia. Didst thou hear these verses?   165

Rosalind. O yes, I heard them all, and more too; for some of them had in them more feet than the verses would bear.

Celia. That's no matter. The feet might bear the verses.   170

Rosalind. Ay, but the feet were lame and could not bear themselves without the verse, and therefore stood lamely in the verse.

145 **wide enlarg'd** in fullest manifestation. 147 **Helen's** Helen of Troy, the immediate cause of the Trojan War. 148 **Cleopatra's** queen of Egypt, mistress of Caesar and Antony. 149 **Atalanta's** Grecian huntress famed for fleetness of foot. 150 **Lucretia's** Roman woman dishonored by Tarquin. 152 **synod** council. 157 **Jupiter** N. 163 **bag and baggage** equipment (a military term). 164 **scrip and scrippage** a wallet and its contents.

Celia. But didst thou hear without wondering how thy name should be hang'd and carved upon these trees? 176

Rosalind. I was seven of the nine days out of the wonder before you came; for look here what I found on a palm tree. I was never so berhym'd since Pythagoras' time that I was an Irish rat, which I can hardly remember. 181

Celia. Trow you who hath done this?

Rosalind. Is it a man?

Celia. And a chain that you once wore—about his neck. Change you color? 185

Rosalind. I prithee, who?

Celia. O Lord, Lord, it is a hard matter for friends to meet. But mountains may be remov'd with earthquakes, and so encounter.

Rosalind. Nay, but who is it? 190

Celia. Is it possible?

Rosalind. Nay, I prithee now with most petitionary vehemence, tell me who it is.

Celia. O wonderful, wonderful, and most wonderful wonderful! And yet again wonderful and after that, out of all hooping. 196

Rosalind. Good my complexion! Dost thou think, though I am caparison'd like a man, I have a doublet and hose in my disposition? One inch of delay more is a South Sea of discovery. I prithee, tell me who is it quickly and speak apace. I would thou couldst stammer, that thou mightst pour this conceal'd man out of thy mouth as wine comes out of a narrow-

179 Pythagoras' time N. 180 that when. Irish rat N. 182 Trow know. 192 petitionary vehemence vehement petition. 196 out of all hooping beyond all shouting. 197 Good my complexion N. 198 caparison'd outfitted. 200 South Sea of discovery N. 201 apace with haste.

mouth'd bottle, either too much at once or none at all. I prithee, take the cork out of thy mouth that I may drink thy tidings.   206

Celia. So you may put a man in your belly?

Rosalind. Is he of God's making? What manner of man? Is his head worth a hat? Or his chin worth a beard?   210

Celia. Nay, he hath but a little beard.

Rosalind. Why, God will send more, if the man will be thankful. Let me stay the growth of his beard, if thou delay me not the knowledge of his chin.   214

Celia. It is young Orlando, that tripp'd up the wrastler's heels and your heart, both in an instant.

Rosalind. Nay, but the divell take mocking. Speak sad brow and true maid.

Celia. I'faith, coz, 'tis he.

Rosalind. Orlando?   220

Celia. Orlando.

Rosalind. Alas the day! What shall I do with my doublet and hose? What did he when thou saw'st him? What said he? How look'd he? Wherein went he? What makes he here? Did he ask for me? Where remains he? How parted he with thee? And when shalt thou see him again? Answer me in one word.

Celia. You must borrow me Gargantua's mouth first; 'tis a word too great for any mouth of this age's size. To say 'ay' and 'no' to these particulars is more than to answer in a catechism.   231

Rosalind. But doth he know that I am in this forest and in man's apparel? Looks he as freshly as he did the day he wrastled?   234

217 **Speak . . . maid** speak solemnly and truly. 224 **Wherein went he?** how was he dressed? 228 **Gargantua's mouth** N. 233 **freshly** vigorous.

Celia. It is as easy to count atomies as to resolve the propositions of a lover. But take a taste of my finding him, and relish it with good observance: I found him under a tree, like a dropp'd acorn.

Rosalind. It may well be call'd Jove's tree, when it drops forth such fruit.   240

Celia. Give me audience, good madam.

Rosalind. Proceed.

Celia. There lay he stretch'd along like a wounded knight.   244

Rosalind. Though it be pity to see such a sight, it well becomes the ground.

Celia. Cry 'holla' to the tongue, I prithee; it curvets unseasonably. He was furnish'd like a hunter.

Rosalind. O ominous: he comes to kill my heart.

Celia. I would sing my song without a burthen; thou bring'st me out of tune.   251

Rosalind. Do you not know I am a woman? When I think, I must speak. Sweet, say on.

Enter Orlando and Jaques.

Celia. You bring me out. Soft, comes he not here?

Rosalind. 'Tis he. Slink by and note him.   255

Jaques. I thank you for your company; but, good faith, I had as lief have been myself alone.

Orlando. And so had I; but yet for fashion sake I thank you too for your society.   259

Jaques. God buy you. Let's meet as little as we can.

235 atomies motes. resolve answer. 236 propositions questions. 237 good observance careful attention. 239 Jove's tree N. 240 such F omits. 241 audience attention. 247 'holla' stop. curvets prances. 248 furnish'd dressed. 249 heart with a pun on 'hart.' 250 burthen refrain. 254 bring me out confuse, bring out of tune. 255 note observe. 257 myself alone by myself. 260 buy F contraction of 'be with.'

Orlando. I do desire we may be better strangers.

Jaques. I pray you mar no more trees with writing love songs in their barks.

Orlando. I pray you mar no moe of my verses with reading them ill-favoredly. 265

Jaques. Rosalind is your love's name?

Orlando. Yes, just.

Jaques. I do not like her name.

Orlando. There was no thought of pleasing you when she was christen'd. 270

Jaques. What stature is she of?

Orlando. Just as high as my heart.

Jaques. You are full of pretty answers. Have you not been acquainted with goldsmiths' wives and conn'd them out of rings? 275

Orlando. Not so. But I answer your right painted cloth, from whence you have studied your questions.

Jaques. You have a nimble wit; I think 'twas made of Atalanta's heels. Will you sit down with me? And we two will rail against our mistress, the World, and all our misery. 281

Orlando. I will chide no breather in the world but myself, against whom I know most faults.

Jaques. The worst fault you have is to be in love.

Orlando. 'Tis a fault I will not change for your best virtue. I am weary of you. 286

Jaques. By my troth, I was seeking for a fool when I found you.

Orlando. He is drown'd in the brook. Look but in and you shall see him. 290

Jaques. There I shall see mine own figure.

264 **moe** more. 265 **ill-favoredly** incorrectly. 267 **just** exactly.
274 **goldsmiths' wives . . . rings** N. 276 **right** regular. **painted cloth** N. 279 **Atalanta's heels** N. 282 **breather** living person.

Orlando. Which I take to be either a fool or a cipher.

Jaques. I'll tarry no longer with you. Farewell,
good Signior Love.   295

Orlando. I am glad of your departure. Adieu, good
Monsieur Melancholy.   [*Exit Jaques.*]

Rosalind. I will speak to him like a saucy lacky and
under that habit play the knave with him. Do you
hear, forester?   300

Orlando. Very well. What would you?

Rosalind. I pray you, what is't o'clock?

Orlando. You should ask me what time o' day.
There's no clock in the forest.   304

Rosalind. Then there is no true lover in the forest,
else sighing every minute and groaning every hour
would detect the lazy foot of Time as well as a
clock.

Orlando. And why not the swift foot of Time? Had
not that been as proper?   310

Rosalind. By no means, sir. Time travels in divers
paces with divers persons. I'll tell you who Time
ambles withal, who Time trots withal, who Time
gallops withal, and who he stands still withal.

Orlando. I prithee, who does he trot withal?   315

Rosalind. Marry, he trots hard with a young maid
between the contract of her marriage and the day
it is solemniz'd. If the interim be but a sennight
Time's pace is so hard that it seems the length of
seven year.   320

Orlando. Who ambles Time withal?

Rosalind. With a priest that lacks Latin and a

292 **cipher** zero. 299 **under that habit** in that guise. 307 **detec**
show. 311 **divers** different. 313 **withal** with. 318 **sennight** a week
(seven nights).

56

rich man that hath not the gout; for the one sleeps easily because he cannot study, and the other lives merrily because he feels no pain: the one lacking the burthen of lean and wasteful learning, the other knowing no burthen of heavy tedious penury. These Time ambles withal.

Orlando. Who doth he gallop withal? 329

Rosalind. With a thief to the gallows. For though he go as softly as foot can fall, he thinks himself too soon there.

Orlando. Who stays it still withal?

Rosalind. With lawyers in the vacation; for they sleep between term and term, and then they perceive not how Time moves. 336

Orlando. Where dwell you, pretty youth?

Rosalind. With this shepherdess, my sister, here in the skirts of the forest, like fringe upon a petticoat.

Orlando. Are you native of this place? 340

Rosalind. As the cony that you see dwell where she is kindled.

Orlando. Your accent is something finer than you could purchase in so removed a dwelling. 344

Rosalind. I have been told so of many. But, indeed, an old religious uncle of mine taught me to speak, who was in his youth an inland man—one that knew courtship too well, for there he fell in love. I have heard him read many lectors against it, and I thank God I am not a woman, to be touch'd with so many giddy offences as he hath generally tax'd their whole sex withal.

Orlando. Can you remember any of the principal evils that he laid to the charge of women? 354

Rosalind. There were none principal. They were all like one another as halfpence are, every one fault seeming monstrous till his fellow fault came to match it.

Orlando. I prithee, recount some of them. 359

Rosalind. No, I will not cast away my physic but on those that are sick. There is a man haunts the forest that abuses our young plants with carving 'Rosalind' on their barks, hangs odes upon hawthornes and elegies on brambles—all, forsooth, deifying the name of Rosalind. If I could meet that fancy-monger, I would give him some good counsel, for he seems to have the quotidian of love upon him.

Orlando. I am he that is so love-shak'd. I pray you, tell me your remedy. 369

Rosalind. There is none of my uncle's marks upon you. He taught me how to know a man in love; in which cage of rushes I am sure you are not prisoner.

Orlando. What were his marks?

Rosalind. A lean cheek, which you have not; a blue eye and sunken, which you have not; an unquestionable spirit, which you have not; a beard neglected, which you have not. But I pardon you for that for, simply, your having in beard is a younger brother's revenue. Then your hose should be ungarter'd, your bonnet unbanded, your sleeve unbutton'd, your shoe

366 **fancy-monger** dealer in love. 367 **quotidian** an ague, a daily fever. 372 **cage of rushes** unsubstantial prison. 374 **blue eye** i.e. with dark circles under it. 375 **unquestionable** unwilling to talk. 378 **simply** to tell the truth. **having in beard** the extent of your beard. 379 **revenue** inheritance.

untied, and every thing about you demonstrating a careless desolation. But you are no such man: you are rather point device in your accoustrements, as loving yourself, than seeming the lover of any other.

Orlando. Fair youth, I would I could make thee believe I love. 386

Rosalind. Me believe it? You may as soon make her that you love believe it, which I warrant she is apter to do than to confess she does. That is one of the points in the which women still give the lie to their consciences. But, in good sooth, are you he that hangs the verses on the trees, wherein Rosalind is so admired?

Orlando. I swear to thee, youth, by the white hand of Rosalind, I am that he, that unfortunate he. 395

Rosalind. But are you so much in love as your rhymes speak?

Orlando. Neither rhyme nor reason can express how much. 399

Rosalind. Love is merely a madness and, I tell you, deserves as well a dark house and a whip as madmen do. And the reason why they are not so punish'd and cured is that the lunacy is so ordinary that the whippers are in love too. Yet I profess curing it by counsel. 405

Orlando. Did you ever cure any so?

Rosalind. Yes, one, and in this manner: he was to imagine me his love, his mistress, and I set him every day to woo me. At which time would I—being

---

382 **careless desolation** depression making one unconcerned with personal appearance. 383 **point device** extremely precise. **accoustrements** accouterments, clothes. 388 **apter** readier. 391 **sooth** truth. 400 **merely** absolutely. 401 **dark house** N. 404 **profess** claim.

but a moonish youth—grieve, be effeminate, changeable, longing and liking, proud, fantastical, apish,
shallow, inconstant, full of tears, full of smiles; for
every passion something, and for no passion truly
anything, as boys and women are for the most part
cattle of this color. Would now like him, now loathe
him; then entertain him, then forswear him; now
weep for him, then spit at him; that I drave my
suitor from his mad humor of love to a living humor
of madness, which was to forswear the full stream of
the world and to live in a nook merely monastic. And
thus I cur'd him, and this way will I take upon me
to wash your liver as clean as a sound sheep's heart,
that there shall not be one spot of love in't.

Orlando. I would not be cured, youth.   424

Rosalind. I would cure you, if you would but call
me Rosalind, and come every day to my cote and
woo me.

Orlando. Now, by the faith of my love, I will. Tell
me where it is.   429

Rosalind. Go with me to it, and I'll show it you.
And by the way you shall tell me where in the forest
you live. Will you go?

Orlando. With all my heart, good youth.

Rosalind. Nay, you must call me Rosalind. Come,
sister. Will you go?   *Exeunt.*   435

410 moonish changeable. 411 fantastical capricious. apish frivo-
lous. 417 that so that. 418 humor condition. 422 liver N.

SCENE 3

Enter Clown [Touchstone], Audrey, and Jaques.

Touchstone. Come apace, good Audrey. I will fetch up your goats, Audrey. And how, Audrey, am I the man yet? Doth my simple feature content you?

Audrey. Your features! Lord warrant us, what features? 5

Touchstone. I am here with thee and thy goats as the most capricious poet, honest Ovid, was among the Goths.

Jaques [aside]. O knowledge ill-inhabited, worse than Jove in a thatch'd house. 10

Touchstone. When a man's verses cannot be understood, nor a man's good wit seconded with the forward child, Understanding, it strikes a man more dead than a great reckoning in a little room. Truly, I would the gods had made thee poetical. 15

Audrey. I do not know what poetical is. Is it honest in deed and word? Is it a true thing?

Touchstone. No, truly, for the truest poetry is the most feigning, and lovers are given to poetry. And what they swear in poetry may be said, as lovers, they do feign. 21

Audrey. Do you wish then that the gods had made me poetical?

Touchstone. I do truly, for thou swear'st to me thou art honest. Now if thou wert a poet, I might have some hope thou didst feign. 26

Come apace hurry along. 3 **feature** face and figure N. 4 **warrant** protect. 7 **capricious** N. 8 **Goths** N. 9 **ill-inhabited** poorly housed. 10 **Jove** Jupiter or Zeus, ruler of the gods. 14 **reckoning . . . room** N. 16 **honest** respectable.

Audrey. Would you not have me honest?

Touchstone. No, truly, unless thou wert hard favor'd. For honesty coupled to beauty is to have
honey a sauce to sugar.   30

Jaques [*aside*]. A material fool.

Audrey. Well, I am not fair, and therefore I pray
the gods make me honest.

Touchstone. Truly, and to cast away honesty upon
a foul slut were to put good meat into an unclean
dish.   36

Audrey. I am not a slut, though I thank the gods I
am foul.

Touchstone. Well, praised be the gods for thy foulness; sluttishness may come hereafter. But be it as it
may be, I will marry thee, and to that end I have
been with Sir Oliver Martext, the vicar of the next
village, who hath promis'd to meet me in this place
of the forest and to couple us.

Jaques [*aside*]. I would fain see this meeting.   45

Audrey. Well, the gods give us joy.

Touchstone. Amen. A man may, if he were of fear-
ful heart, stagger in this attempt; for here we have
no temple but the wood, no assembly but horn-beasts.
But what though? Courage. As horns are odious,
they are necessary. It is said many a man knows no
end of his goods. Right. Many a man has good horns
and knows no end of them. Well, that is the dowry of
his wife; 'tis none of his own getting. Horns? Even
so. Poor men alone? No, no. The noblest deer hath
them as huge as the rascal. Is the single man therefore blessed? No. As a wall'd town is more worthier

27 **honest** chaste. 28 **hard favor'd** ugly. 31 **material** full of ideas.
35 **foul** ugly. 42 **Sir** N. 44 **couple** join, marry. 48 **heart** N. 49 **horn-
beasts** N. 50 **But what though?** but what of that? 56 **rascal** a
young or inferior deer.

than a village, so is the forehead of a married man
more honorable than the bare brow of a bachelor.
And by how much defense is better than no skill, by
so much is a horn more precious than to want.   61

Enter Sir Oliver Martext.

Here comes Sir Oliver. Sir Oliver Martext, you are
well met. Will you dispatch us here under this tree,
or shall we go with you to your chapel?   64
  Sir Oliver. Is there none here to give the woman?
  Touchstone. I will not take her on gift of any man.
  Sir Oliver. Truly, she must be given or the marriage
is not lawful.
  Jaques. Proceed, proceed. I'll give her.   69
  Touchstone. Good even, good Master What-ye-
call't. How do you, sir? You are very well met. Goddild you for your last company. I am very glad to
see you. Even a toy in hand here, sir. Nay, pray be
cover'd.
  Jaques. Will you be married, motley?   75
  Touchstone. As the ox hath his bow, sir, the horse
his curb, and the falcon her bells, so man hath his
desires; and as pigeons bill, so wedlock would be
nibbling.   79
  Jaques. And will you, being a man of your breeding,
be married under a bush like a beggar? Get you to
church and have a good priest that can tell you
what marriage is. This fellow will but join you together as they join wainscote; then one of you will
prove a shrunk panel and, like green timber, warp,
warp.   86
  Touchstone. I am not in the mind but I were better

61 **want** lack. 63 **dispatch** i.e. marry. 70 **Master What-ye-call't** N.
71 **Goddild** God reward you. 73 **toy** trifling matter. **be cover'd**
put on your hat. 75 **motley** fool. 76 **bow** yoke.

63

to be married of him than of another, for he is not
like to marry me well. And not being well married, it
will be a good excuse for me hereafter to leave my
wife.   91

Jaques. Go thou with me and let me counsel thee.

Touchstone. Come, sweet Audrey.
We must be married, or we must live in bawdry.
Farewell, good Master Oliver: not   95

> *O sweet Oliver,*
> *O brave Oliver,*
> *Leave me not behind thee.*

but

> *Wind away,*   100
> *Be gone, I say!*
> *I will not to wedding with thee.*

Sir Oliver. 'Tis no matter. Ne'er a fantastical knave
of them all shall flout me out of my calling.

Exeunt.

SCENE 4

Enter Rosalind and Celia.

Rosalind. Never talk to me; I will weep.

Celia. Do, I prithee. But yet have the grace to consider that tears do not become a man.

Rosalind. But have I not cause to weep?   4

Celia. As good cause as one would desire. Therefore
weep.

Rosalind. His very hair is of the dissembling color.

Celia. Something browner than Judas'. Marry, his
kisses are Judas' own children.

94 bawdry sin. 96 O sweet Oliver N. 100 Wind away go away.
104 flout jeer. 7 dissembling color N.

Rosalind. I' faith, his hair is of a good color. 10

Celia. An excellent color. Your chestnut was ever the only color.

Rosalind. And his kissing is as full of sanctity as the touch of holy bread. 14

Celia. He hath bought a pair of cast lips of Diana. A nun of winter's sisterhood kisses not more religiously; the very ice of chastity is in them.

Rosalind. But why did he swear he would come this morning, and comes not?

Celia. Nay, certainly there is no truth in him. 20

Rosalind. Do you think so?

Celia. Yes. I think he is not a pickpurse nor a horse-stealer, but for his verity in love, I do think him as concave as a covered goblet or a worm-eaten nut. 25

Rosalind. Not true in love?

Celia. Yes, when he is in. But I think he is not in.

Rosalind. You have heard him swear downright he was. 29

Celia. 'Was' is not 'is.' Besides, the oath of a lover is no stronger than the word of a tapster; they are both the confirmer of false reckonings. He attends here in the forest on the Duke your father.

Rosalind. I met the Duke yesterday and had much question with him. He ask'd me of what parentage I was; I told him of as good as he. So he laugh'd and let me go. But what talk we of fathers when there is such a man as Orlando?

---

15 **cast** cast off. **lips of Diana** Diana was the goddess of chastity. 16 **winter's sisterhood** i.e. the bond of chastity. 23 **verity** truth. 24 **concave** hollow, insincere. 30 **a** F omits. 31 **tapster** tavern waiter. 32 **reckonings** accounts, charges. 35 **question** conversation.

Celia. O, that's a brave man! He writes brave
verses, speaks brave words, swears brave oaths, and
breaks them bravely—quite traverse athwart the
heart of his lover, as a puisny tilter that spurs his
horse but on one side breaks his staff like a noble
goose. But all's brave that youth mounts and folly
guides. Who comes here?   45

Enter Corin.

Corin. Mistress and master, you have oft inquired
After the shepherd that complain'd of love,
Who you saw sitting by me on the turf
Praising the proud disdainful shepherdess
That was his mistress.
Celia.   Well, and what of him?   50
Corin. If you will see a pageant truly play'd
Between the pale complexion of true love
And the red glow of scorn and proud disdain,
Go hence a little and I shall conduct you,
If you will mark it.
Rosalind.   O, come, let us remove.   55
The sight of lovers feedeth those in love.
Bring us to this sight, and you shall say
I'll prove a busy actor in their play.   *Exeunt.*

SCENE 5

Enter Silvius and Phebe.

Silvius. Sweet Phebe, do not scorn me. Do not,
     Phebe.

39 **brave** fine. 41 **traverse athwart** N. 42 **puisny** insignificant,
incompetent (pronounced 'puny'). 52 **pale complexion** N.
55 **mark** observe. **remove** depart.

Say that you love me not, but say not so
In bitterness. The common executioner,
Whose heart th' accustom'd sight of death makes
    hard,
Falls not the ax upon the humbled neck   5
But first begs pardon. Will you sterner be
Than he that dies and lives by bloody drops?

Enter Rosalind, Celia, and Corin.

  Phebe. I would not be thy executioner.
I fly thee, for I would not injure thee.
Thou tell'st me there is murder in mine eye.   10
'Tis pretty, sure, and very probable
That eyes, that are the frail'st and softest things,
Who shut their coward gates on atomies,
Should be called tyrants, butchers, murtherers.
Now I do frown on thee with all my heart,   15
And if mine eyes can wound, now let them kill thee.
Now counterfeit to swound. Why, now fall down!
Or if thou canst not, O for shame, for shame.
Lie not, to say mine eyes are murtherers.
Now show the wound mine eye hath made in thee.   20
Scratch thee but with a pin and there remains
Some scar of it; lean but upon a rush,
The cicatrice and capable impressure
Thy palm some moment keeps. But now mine eyes,
Which I have darted at thee, hurt thee not;   25
Nor I am sure there is no force in eyes
That can do hurt.
  Silvius.   O dear Phebe,
If ever, as that ever may be near,

5 **Falls** lets fall. 7 **dies and lives** makes his living. 14 **murtherers**
murderers. 17 **counterfeit** pretend. **swound** swoon. 22 **but** F
omits. 23 **cicatrice** impression. **capable impressure** firm imprint.

You meet in some fresh cheek the power of fancy,
Then shall you know the wounds invisible   30
That Love's keen arrows make.
  Phebe.   But till that time
Come not thou near me. And when that time comes,
Afflict me with thy mocks; pity me not,
As till that time I shall not pity thee.
  Rosalind. And why, I pray you? Who might be
      your mother   35
That you insult, exult, and all at once,
Over the wretched? What, though you have no
    beauty—
As, by my faith, I see no more in you
Than without candle may go dark to bed—
Must you be therefore proud and pitiless?   40
Why, what means this? Why do you look on me?
I see no more in you than in the ordinary
Of Nature's sale-work. 'Od's my little life,
I think she means to tangle my eyes too.
No, faith, proud mistress, hope not after it;   45
'Tis not your inky brows, your black silk hair,
Your bugle eyeballs, nor your cheek of cream
That can entame my spirits to your worship.
You foolish shepherd, wherefore do you follow her
Like foggy south, puffing with wind and rain?   50
You are a thousand times a properer man
Than she a woman. 'Tis such fools as you
That makes the world full of ill-favor'd children.
'Tis not her glass but you that flatters her,
And out of you she sees herself more proper   55

29 **fancy** love. 39 **candle** . . . **bed** N. 43 **sale-work** product of poor quality. **'Od's** God save. 47 **bugle** a black glass bead, here meaning 'black.' 48 **entame** subdue. **to your worship** to worship you. 50 **south** south wind N. 51 **properer** handsomer. 54 **glass** mirror.

Than any of her lineaments can show her.
But, mistress, know yourself. Down on your knees
And thank heaven, fasting, for a good man's love.
For I must tell you friendly in your ear:
Sell when you can; you are not for all markets.   60
Cry the man mercy, love him, take his offer.
Foul is most foul, being foul to be a scoffer.
So take her to thee, shepherd. Fare you well.
    Phebe. Sweet youth, I pray you, chide a year to-
        gether.
I had rather hear you chide than this man woo.   65
    Rosalind. He's falne in love with your foulness, and
she'll fall in love with my anger. If it be so, as fast
as she answers thee with frowning looks, I'll sauce
her with bitter words. Why look you so upon me?
    Phebe. For no ill will I bear you.   70
    Rosalind. I pray you, do not fall in love with me,
For I am falser than vows made in wine.
Besides, I like you not. If you will know my house,
'Tis at the tuft of olives here hard by.
Will you go, sister? Shepherd, ply her hard.   75
Come, sister. Shepherdess, look on him better
And be not proud, though all the world could see
None could be so abus'd in sight as he.
Come, to our flock.

        Exeunt [*Rosalind, Celia, Corin*].
    Phebe. Dead shepherd, now I find thy saw of might:
'Whoever lov'd that lov'd not at first sight?'   81
    Silvius. Sweet Phebe.
    Phebe. Hah! What say'st thou, Silvius?
    Silvius. Sweet Phebe, pity me.

61 **Cry . . . mercy** beg for mercy. 62 **Foul . . . scoffer** N. 64
together on end. 65 **I had** to be read 'I'd.' 66 **falne** fall'n.
68 **sauce** rebuke. 76 **better** more kindly. 78 **abus'd in sight**
deceived by eyesight. 80 **Dead shepherd** N.

69

Phebe. Why, I am sorry for thee, gentle Silvius. 85
Silvius. Wherever sorrow is, relief would be.
If you do sorrow at my grief in love,
By giving love your sorrow and my grief
Were both extermin'd. 89
Phebe. Thou hast my love. Is not that neighborly?
Silvius. I would have you.
Phebe.   Why, that were covetous-
         ness.
Silvius, the time was that I hated thee,
And yet it is not that I bear thee love.
But since that thou canst talk of love so well,
Thy company, which erst was irksome to me, 95
I will endure; and I'll employ thee too.
But do not look for further recompense
Than thine own gladness that thou art employ'd.
Silvius. So holy and so perfect is my love,
And I in such a poverty of grace, 100
That I shall think it a most plenteous crop
To glean the broken ears after the man
That the main harvest reaps. Loose now and then
A scatt'red smile, and that I'll live upon.
Phebe. Know'st thou the youth that spoke to me
         erewhile? 105
Silvius. Not very well. But I have met him oft,
And he hath bought the cottage and the bounds
That the old Carlot once was master of.
Phebe. Think not I love him, though I ask for him.
'Tis but a peevish boy, yet he talks well. 110
But what care I for words? Yet words do well
When he that speaks them pleases those that hear.

89 **extermin'd** banished. 90 **neighborly** N. 95 **erst** at first. 100 **poverty of grace** lack of favor. 104 **scatt'red** stray. 105 **erewhile** a little while ago; F *yerewhile.* 107 **bounds** acreage. 108 **Carlot** N.

It is a pretty youth—not very pretty.
But sure he's proud, and yet his pride becomes him.
He'll make a proper man: the best thing in him   115
Is his complexion. And faster than his tongue
Did make offense his eyes did heal it up.
He is not very tall, yet for his years he's tall.
His leg is but so-so, and yet 'tis well.
There was a pretty redness in his lip,   120
A little riper and more lusty red
Than that mix'd in his cheek. 'Twas just the differ-
    ence
Betwixt the constant red and mingled damask.
There be some women, Silvius, had they mark'd him
In parcels as I did, would have gone near   125
To fall in love with him. But for my part,
I love him not nor hate him not; and yet
I have more cause to hate him than to love him,
For what had he to do to chide at me?   129
He said mine eyes were black and my hair black,
And, now I am remb'red, scorn'd at me.
I marvel why I answer'd not again.
But that's all one: omittance is no quittance.
I'll write to him a very tanting letter,
And thou shalt bear it. Wilt thou, Silvius?   135
  Silvius. Phebe, with all my heart.
    Phebe.   I'll write it
    straight.
The matter's in my head and in my heart:
I will be bitter with him and passing short.
Go with me, Silvius.   *Exeunt.*

123 **constant** uniform. **mingled damask** a mixture of red and
white, like the damask rose. 124 **be** are. 125 **In parcels** bit by bit.
128 **I** F omits. 131 **I am remb'red** I recall. 133 **omittance** . . .
quittance N. 134 **tanting** taunting. 138 **passing short** exceed-
ingly curt.

Act IV

SCENE 1

Enter Rosalind, and Celia, and Jaques.

Jaques. I prithee, pretty youth, let me be better acquainted with thee.

Rosalind. They say you are a melancholy fellow.

Jaques. I am so. I do love it better than laughing.

Rosalind. Those that are in extremity of either are abominable fellows, and betray themselves to every modern censure worse than drunkards.

Jaques. Why, 'tis good to be sad and say nothing.

Rosalind. Why, then 'tis good to be a post. 9

Jaques. I have neither the scholar's melancholy, which is emulation; nor the musician's, which is fantastical; nor the courtier's, which is proud; nor the soldier's, which is ambitious; nor the lawyer's, which is politic; nor the lady's, which is nice; nor the lover's, which is all these. But it is a melancholy of mine own, compounded of many simples, extracted from many objects, and indeed the sundry contemplation of my travels, in which my often rumination wraps me in a most humorous sadness. 19

Rosalind. A traveler! By my faith, you have great

---

1 **be** F omits. 8 **sad** here with two meanings: 'melancholy' and 'heavy.' 11 **emulation** envy. 14 **politic** crafty. **nice** delicate. 16 **simples** herbs, ingredients.

reason to be sad. I fear you have sold your own lands to see other men's. Then to have seen much and to have nothing is to have rich eyes and poor hands.

Jaques. Yes, I have gain'd my experience.   25

Enter Orlando.

Rosalind. And your experience makes you sad. I had rather have a fool to make me merry than experience to make me sad, and to travel for it too.

Orlando. Good day and happiness, dear Rosalind.

Jaques. Nay, then, God buy you, and you talk in blank verse.   31

Rosalind. Farewell, Monsieur Traveler. Look you lisp and wear strange suits, disable all the benefits of your own country, be out of love with your nativity, and almost chide God for making you that countenance you are; or I will scarce think you have swam in a gundello. [*Exit Jaques.*] Why, how now, Orlando? Where have you been all this while? You a lover? And you serve me such another trick, never come in my sight more.   40

Orlando. My fair Rosalind, I come within an hour of my promise.

Rosalind. Break an hour's promise in love? He that will divide a minute into a thousand parts and break but a part of the thousand part of a minute in the affairs of love, it may be said of him that Cupid hath clapp'd him o' th' shoulder. But I'll warrant him heart-whole.

30 **buy** be with. **and** an (if). 33 **lisp** talk in an affected manner. **disable** disparage. 34 **nativity** birthplace. 36 **swam . . . gundello** ridden in a gondola, i.e. been to Venice. 39 **And** an (if). 47 **clapp'd** seized on the shoulder as if to arrest.

Orlando. Pardon me, dear Rosalind.   49

Rosalind. Nay. And you be so tardy, come no more in my sight; I had as lief be woo'd of a snail.

Orlando. Of a snail?

Rosalind. Ay, of a snail. For though he comes slowly, he carries his house on his head—a better jointure, I think, than you make a woman. Besides, he brings his destiny with him.   56

Orlando. What's that?

Rosalind. Why, horns; which such as you are fain to be beholding to your wives for. But he comes armed in his fortune, and prevents the slander of his wife.   61

Orlando. Virtue is no horn-maker, and my Rosalind is virtuous.

Rosalind. And I am your Rosalind.   64

Celia. It pleases him to call you so. But he hath a Rosalind of a better leer than you.

Rosalind. Come, woo me, woo me; for now I am in a holiday humor and like enough to consent. What would you say to me now, and I were your very very Rosalind?   70

Orlando. I would kiss before I spoke.

Rosalind. Nay, you were better speak first; and when you were gravel'd for lack of matter, you might take occasion to kiss. Very good orators, when they are out, they will spit; and for lovers lacking— God warn us—matter, the cleanliest shift is to kiss.

Orlando. How if the kiss be denied?

50 **And** an (if). 51 **of** by. 55 **jointure** marriage portion. 58 **horns** N. 59 **beholding** beholden. 60 **armed** i.e. with horns. 62 **horn-maker** cuckold-maker. 66 **leer** appearance. 69 **and** an (if). 73 **gravel'd** nonplussed. 75 **out** out of material. 76 **God warn us** God warrant (protect) us. **cleanliest shift** cleverest device.

Rosalind. Then she puts you to entreaty, and there begins new matter.   79

Orlando. Who could be out, being before his beloved mistress?

Rosalind. Marry, that should you if I were your mistress, or I should think my honesty ranker than my wit.

Orlando. What of my suit?   85

Rosalind. Not out of your apparel, and yet out of your suit. Am I not your Rosalind?

Orlando. I take some joy to say you are, because I would be talking of her.   89

Rosalind. Well, in her person, I say I will not have you.

Orlando. Then, in mine own person, I die.

Rosalind. No, faith, die by attorney. The poor world is almost six thousand years old, and in all this time there was not any man died in his own person, *videlicet*, in a love cause. Troilus had his brains dash'd out with a Grecian club, yet he did what he could to die before; and he is one of the patterns of love. Leander, he would have liv'd many a fair year though Hero had turn'd nun, if it had not been for a hot midsummer night; for, good youth, he went but forth to wash him in the Hellespont, and being taken with the cramp, was drown'd; and the foolish chroniclers of that age found it was 'Hero of Cestos.' But these are all lies. Men have died from time to time and worms have eaten them, but not for love.   106

Orlando. I would not have my right Rosalind of this mind, for I protest her frown might kill me.

83 **ranker** more flourishing. 85 **suit** N. 93 **by attorney** by proxy. 95 **videlicet** namely. 96 **Troilus** N. 98 **patterns** models. 99 **Leander** N. 104 **found** gave the verdict (in a legal sense). 107 **right** true.

Rosalind. By this hand, it will not kill a fly. But come. Now I will be your Rosalind in a more coming-on disposition; and ask me what you will, I will grant it.

Orlando. Then love me, Rosalind.

Rosalind. Yes, faith, will I—Fridays and Saturdays and all. 115

Orlando. And wilt thou have me?

Rosalind. Ay, and twenty such.

Orlando. What sayest thou?

Rosalind. Are you not good?

Orlando. I hope so. 120

Rosalind. Why then, can one desire too much of a good thing? Come, sister, you shall be the priest and marry us. Give me your hand, Orlando. What do you say, sister?

Orlando. Pray thee, marry us. 125

Celia. I cannot say the words.

Rosalind. You must begin, 'Will you, Orlando . . .'

Celia. Go to. Will you, Orlando, have to wife this Rosalind?

Orlando. I will. 130

Rosalind. Ay, but when?

Orlando. Why, now. As fast as she can marry us.

Rosalind. Then you must say, 'I take thee, Rosalind, for wife.'

Orlando. I take thee, Rosalind, for wife. 135

Rosalind. I might ask you for your commission, but I do take thee, Orlando, for my husband. There's a girl goes before the priest, and certainly a woman's thought runs before her actions.

Orlando. So do all thoughts; they are wing'd. 140

---

136 **commission** authority. 138 **goes before** anticipates.

Rosalind. Now tell me how long you would have her after you have possess'd her?

Orlando. For ever and a day.

Rosalind. Say 'a day' without the 'ever.' No, no, Orlando. Men are April when they woo, December when they wed; maids are May when they are maids, but the sky changes when they are wives. I will be more jealous of thee than a Barbary cock-pigeon over his hen, more clamorous than a parrot against rain, more new-fangled than an ape, more giddy in my desires than a monkey. I will weep for nothing, like Diana in the fountain, and I will do that when you are dispos'd to be merry. I will laugh like a hyen, and that when thou art inclin'd to sleep.

Orlando. But will my Rosalind do so?   155

Rosalind. By my life, she will do as I do.

Orlando. O, but she is wise.

Rosalind. Or else she could not have the wit to do this. The wiser, the waywarder. Make the doors upon a woman's wit, and it will out at the casement; shut that, and 'twill out at the keyhole; stop that, 'twill fly with the smoke out at the chimney.

Orlando. A man that had a wife with such a wit, he might say, 'Wit, whether wilt?'   164

Rosalind. Nay, you might keep that check for it till you met your wive's wit going to your neighbor's bed.

Orlando. And what wit could wit have to excuse that?

Rosalind. Marry, to say she came to seek you there. You shall never take her without her answer unless you take her without her tongue. O, that woman that

148 **Barbary** Oriental. 149 **against** in expectation of. 150 **new-fangled** fond of novelty. **giddy** capricious. 152 **Diana** N. 153 **hyen** hyena. 159 **Make** shut. 164 **'Wit . . . wilt?'** N. 165 **check** rebuke. 166 **wive's** wife's, an old genitive.

cannot make her fault her husband's occasion, let her
never nurse her child herself, for she will breed it like
a fool.   174

Orlando. For these two hours, Rosalind, I will leave
thee.

Rosalind. Alas, dear love, I cannot lack thee two
hours.

Orlando. I must attend the Duke at dinner. By two
o'clock I will be with thee again.   180

Rosalind. Ay, go your ways, go your ways. I knew
what you would prove; my friends told me as much,
and I thought no less. That flattering tongue of
yours won me. 'Tis but one cast away, and so come
death. Two o'clock is your hour.   185

Orlando. Ay, sweet Rosalind.

Rosalind. By my troth, and in good earnest, and so
God mend me, and by all pretty oaths that are not
dangerous, if you break one jot of your promise or
come one minute behind your hour, I will think you
the most pathetical break-promise and the most hollow lover and the most unworthy of her you call
Rosalind that may be chosen out of the gross band
of the unfaithful. Therefore beware my censure and
keep your promise.   195

Orlando. With no less religion than if thou wert
indeed my Rosalind. So adieu.

Rosalind. Well, Time is the old justice that ex-
amines all such offenders, and let Time try. Adieu.
                                         Exit [*Orlando*].

Celia. You have simply misus'd our sex in your love

---

172 **occasion** N. 177 **lack** do without. 188 **mend me** change my
fortune. 191 **pathetical** pitiable. 193 **gross** whole. 194 **censure**
condemnation. 196 **religion** fidelity. 200 **simply** completely.
misus'd abused.

prate. We must have your doublet and hose pluck'd over your head and show the world what the bird hath done to her own nest.

Rosalind. O coz, coz, coz, my pretty little coz, that thou didst know how many fathom deep I am in love! But it cannot be sounded; my affection hath an unknown bottom, like the Bay of Portugal.

Celia. Or rather bottomless—that as fast as you pour affection in, it runs out.   209

Rosalind. No; that same wicked bastard of Venus that was begot of thought, conceiv'd of spleen, and born of madness, that blind rascally boy that abuses everyone's eyes because his own are out—let him be judge how deep I am in love. I'll tell thee, Aliena, I cannot be out of sight of Orlando. I'll go find a shadow and sigh till he come.   216

Celia. And I'll sleep.   *Exeunt.*

SCENE 2

Enter Jaques and Lords, Foresters.

Jaques. Which is he that killed the deer?

Lord. Sir, it was I.

Jaques. Let's present him to the Duke like a Roman conqueror, and it would do well to set the deer's horns upon his head for a branch of victory. Have you no song, forester, for this purpose?   6

Lord. Yes, sir.

Jaques. Sing it. 'Tis no matter how it be in tune, so it make noise enough.   *Music.*

202 bird . . . nest N. 210 **bastard of Venus** N. 211 **thought** melancholy. **spleen** impulse.

Song

What shall he have that kill'd the deer?   10
His leathern skin and horns to wear.
Then sing him home. The rest shall bear
    This burthen:

Take thou no scorn to wear the horn.
It was a crest ere thou wast born.   15
    Thy father's father wore it,
    And thy father bore it.
The horn, the horn, the lusty horn
Is not a thing to laugh to scorn.

Exeunt.

SCENE 3

Enter Rosalind and Celia.

Rosalind. How say you now? Is it not past two
o'clock? And here much Orlando.

Celia. I warrant you, with pure love and troubled
brain   4

Enter Silvius.

he hath tane his bow and arrows and is gone forth to
sleep. Look who comes here.

Silvius. My errand is to you, fair youth.
My gentle Phebe did bid me give you this.
         [Presenting a letter.]
I know not the contents but, as I guess
By the stern brow and waspish action   10
Which she did use as she was writing of it,
It bears an angry tenure. Pardon me,

12 **The rest . . . burthen** N. 19 **laugh to scorn** ridicule. 2 **here
much Orlando** i.e. spoken with irony. 12 **tenure** tenor, purport
(to be read 'tenor').

I am but as a guiltless messenger.

Rosalind. Patience herself would startle at this
    letter
And play the swaggerer. Bear this, bear all.   15
She says I am not fair, that I lack manners;
She calls me proud, and that she could not love me
Were man as rare as Phoenix. 'Od's my will,
Her love is not the hare that I do hunt.
Why writes she so to me? Well, shepherd, well?   20
This is a letter of your own device.

Silvius. No, I protest. I know not the contents;
Phebe did write it.

Rosalind.   Come, come, you are a fool,
And turn'd into the extremity of love.
I saw her hand: she has a leathern hand,   25
A freestone colored hand. I verily did think
That her old gloves were on, but 'twas her hands.
She has a housewive's hand; but that's no matter.
I say she never did invent this letter.
This is a man's invention and his hand.   30

Silvius. Sure it is hers.

Rosalind. Why, 'tis a boisterous and a cruel style,
A style for challengers. Why, she defies me,
Like Turk to Christian. Women's gentle brain
Could not drop forth such giant rude invention,   35
Such Ethiop words, blacker in their effect
Than in their countenance. Will you hear the letter?

Silvius. So please you, for I never heard it yet;
Yet heard too much of Phebe's cruelty.

18 **Phoenix** N. 24 **turn'd** brought. **the extremity** to be read
'th' extremity.' 26 **freestone colored** the color of brown stone
32 **boisterous** to be read 'boist'rous.' 34 **Turk** N. 35 **giant rude**
extremely rude. 36 **Ethiop** black. 37 **countenance** to be read
'count'nance.'

Rosalind. She Phebes me! Mark how the tyrant writes.   *Read.*

> Art thou God to shepherd turn'd
> That a maiden's heart hath burn'd?

Can a woman rail thus?
Silvius. Call you this railing?

Read.

Rosalind.   Why, thy Godhead laid apart,   45
> Warr'st thou with a woman's heart?

Did you ever hear such railing?

> Whiles the eyes of man did woo me
> That could do no vengeance to me.

Meaning me a beast.   50

> If the scorn of your bright eyne
> Have power to raise such love in mine,
> Alack, in me what strange effect
> Would they work in mild aspect?
> Whiles you chid me, I did love;   55
> How then might your prayers move!
> He that brings this love to thee
> Little knows this love in me.
> And by him seal up thy mind
> Whether that thy youth and kind   60
> Will the faithful offer take
> Of me and all that I can make;
> Or else by him my love deny,
> And then I'll study how to die.

Silvius. Call you this chiding?   65
Celia. Alas, poor shepherd.
Rosalind. Do you pity him? No, he deserves no

40 Phebes treats cruelly, acts like Phebe. 45 **Godhead** divinity. **laid apart** put aside. 51 **eyne** archaic plural of 'eye.' 54 **aspect** stressed — ´ . 59 **seal up thy mind** send under seal. 60 **youth and kind** youthful nature.

82

pity. Wilt thou love such a woman? What, to make
thee an instrument and play false strains upon thee?
Not to be endur'd. Well, go your way to her—for I
see love hath made thee a tame snake—and say this
to her: that if she loves me, I charge her to love thee;
if she will not, I will never have her unless thou entreat for her. If you be a true lover, hence, and not
a word. For here comes more company.   75
                                   Exit Silvius.

                  Enter Oliver.

Oliver. Good morrow, fair ones. Pray you, if you
    know,
Where in the purlieus of this forest stands
A sheepcote fenc'd about with olive trees?
Celia. West of this place, down in the neighbor
    bottom.
The rank of osiers by the murmuring stream,   80
Left on your right hand, brings you to the place.
But at this hour the house doth keep itself;
There's none within.
Oliver. If that an eye may profit by a tongue,
Then should I know you by description: 85
Such garments and such years. 'The boy is fair,
Of female favor, and bestows himself
Like a ripe sister; the woman low
And browner than her brother.' Are not you
The owner of the house I did inquire for?   90
Celia. It is no boast, being ask'd, to say we are.
Oliver. Orlando doth commend him to you both,
And to that youth he calls his Rosalind

77 **purlieus** borders of a forest. 79 **bottom** valley. 80 **osiers** willows.
82 **keep itself** take care of itself (i.e. is empty). 87 **favor** feature.
bestows carries. 88 **ripe** grown up. **low** short.

He sends this bloody napkin. Are you he?   94

   Rosalind. I am. What must we understand by this?

   Oliver. Some of my shame, if you will know of me
What man I am, and how and why and where
This handkercher was stain'd.

   Celia.   I pray you tell it.

   Oliver. When last the young Orlando parted from
     you,
He left a promise to return again   100
Within an hour; and pacing through the forest,
Chewing the food of sweet and bitter fancy,
Lo, what befell! He threw his eye aside,
And mark what object did present itself   104
Under an old oak, whose boughs were moss'd with age
And high top bald with dry antiquity:
A wretched ragged man, o'ergrown with hair,
Lay sleeping on his back. About his neck
A green and gilded snake had wreath'd itself,   109
Who with her head nimble in threats approach'd
The opening of his mouth. But suddenly,
Seeing Orlando, it unlink'd itself
And with indented glides did slip away
Into a bush. Under which bush's shade
A lioness, with udders all drawn dry,   115
Lay couching head on ground, with catlike watch
When that the sleeping man should stir; for 'tis
The royal disposition of that beast
To prey on nothing that doth seem as dead.
This seen, Orlando did approach the man   120
And found it was his brother, his elder brother.

94 **napkin** handkerchief. 98 **handkercher** handkerchief. 103 **threw**
. . . **aside** looked to one side. 105 **old** this word causes an irregu-
lar line but it appears in all folios. 112 **unlink'd** uncoiled. 113
indented winding.

Celia. O, I have heard him speak of that same
    brother,
And he did render him the most unnatural
That liv'd amongst men.
Oliver.   And well he might so do,
For well I know he was unnatural.   125
Rosalind. But to Orlando: did he leave him there,
Food to the suck'd and hungry lioness?
Oliver. Twice did he turn his back and purpos'd so.
But kindness, nobler ever than revenge,
And nature stronger than his just occasion   130
Made him give battle to the lioness,
Who quickly fell before him. In which hurtling
From miserable slumber I awaked.
Celia. Are you his brother?
Rosalind.   Was't you he rescu'd?
Celia. Was't you that did so oft contrive to kill him?
Oliver. 'Twas I, but 'tis not I. I do not shame   136
To tell you what I was, since my conversion
So sweetly tastes, being the thing I am.
Rosalind. But for the bloody napkin?
Oliver.   By and by.
When from the first to last, betwixt us two   140
Tears our recountments had most kindly bath'd,
As how I came into that desert place—
In brief, he led me to the gentle Duke,
Who gave me fresh array and entertainment,
Committing me unto my brother's love;   145
Who led me instantly unto his cave,
There stripp'd himself, and here upon his arm
The lioness had torn some flesh away,
Which all this while had bled. And now he fainted

123 **render** describe. 130 **occasion** opportunity. 132 **hurtling** tumult. 135 **contrive** plot. 141 **recountments** stories.

And cried, in fainting, upon Rosalind.   150
Brief, I recover'd him, bound up his wound,
And after some small space, being strong at heart,
He sent me hither, stranger as I am,
To tell this story that you might excuse
His broken promise; and to give this napkin,   155
Dy'd in his blood, unto the shepherd youth
That he in sport doth call his Rosalind.

                              [*Rosalind faints.*]

Celia. Why, how now, Ganymede, sweet Ganymede!
Oliver. Many will swoon when they do look on blood.
Celia. There is more in it. Cousin Ganymede!   160
Oliver. Look, he recovers.
Rosalind. I would I were at home.
Celia.   We'll lead you
     thither.
I pray you, will you take him by the arm?
Oliver. Be of good cheer, youth. You a man? You
lack a man's heart.   165
Rosalind. I do so, I confess it. Ah, sirrah, a body
would think this was well counterfeited. I pray you
tell your brother how well I counterfeited. Heigh-ho!
Oliver. This was not counterfeit; there is too great
testimony in your complexion that it was a passion
of earnest.   171
Rosalind. Counterfeit, I assure you.
Oliver. Well then, take a good heart and counterfeit to be a man.   174
Rosalind. So I do. But, i' faith, I should have been
a woman by right.
Celia. Come, you look paler and paler. Pray you,
draw homewards. Good sir, go with us.

151 **Brief** briefly. **recover'd** revived. 170 **passion of earnest** a
genuine swoon.

Oliver. That will I, for we must bear answer back how you excuse my brother, Rosalind.   180

Rosalind. I shall devise something, but I pray you commend my counterfeiting to him. Will you go?

Exeunt.

Act V

SCENE 1

Enter Clown [Touchstone] and Audrey.

Touchstone. We shall find a time, Audrey. Patience, gentle Audrey.

Audrey. Faith, the priest was good enough, for all the old gentleman's saying.   4

Touchstone. A most wicked Sir Oliver, Audrey, a most vile Martext. But, Audrey, there is a youth here in the forest lays claim to you.

Audrey. Ay, I know who 'tis. He hath no interest in me in the world. Here comes the man you mean.   9

Enter William.

Touchstone. It is meat and drink to me to see a clown. By my troth, we that have good wits have much to answer for. We shall be flouting; we cannot hold.

William. Good ev'n, Audrey.

Audrey. God ye good ev'n, William.   15

---

11 **clown** rustic. 12 **flouting** mocking. 13 **hold** refrain. 15 **God ye** God give you.

William. And good ev'n to you, sir.

Touchstone. Good ev'n, gentle friend. Cover thy head, cover thy head. Nay, prithee be cover'd. How old are you, friend?

William. Five and twenty, sir.   20

Touchstone. A ripe age. Is thy name William?

William. William, sir.

Touchstone. A fair name. Wast born i' th' forest here?

William. Ay, sir, I thank God.   25

Touchstone. 'Thank God': a good answer. Art rich?

William. Faith, sir, so-so.

Touchstone. 'So-so' is good, very good, very excellent good. And yet it is not; it is but so-so. Art thou wise?   30

William. Ay, sir, I have a pretty wit.

Touchstone. Why, thou say'st well. I do now remember a saying: 'The fool doth think he is wise, but the wise man knows himself to be a fool.' The heathen philosopher, when he had a desire to eat a grape, would open his lips when he put it into his mouth, meaning thereby that grapes were made to eat and lips to open. You do love this maid?

William. I do, sir.   39

Touchstone. Give me your hand. Art thou learned?

William. No, sir.

Touchstone. Then learn this of me: to have is to have. For it is a figure in rhetoric that drink, being pour'd out of a cup into a glass, by filling the one doth empty the other. For all your writers do consent that *ipse* is he; now you are not *ipse*, for I am he.

31 **wit** intelligence. 46 **ipse** he himself (Latin).

William. Which he, sir?

Touchstone. He, sir, that must marry this woman. Therefore, you clown, abandon (which is in the vulgar 'leave') the society (which in the boorish is 'company') of this female (which in the common is 'woman'); which together is, abandon the society of this female. Or, clown, thou perishest; or, to thy better understanding, diest; or, to wit, I kill thee, make thee away, translate thy life into death, thy liberty into bondage. I will deal in poison with thee, or in bastinado, or in steel; I will bandy with thee in faction; I will o'errun thee with policy; I will kill thee a hundred and fifty ways. Therefore tremble and depart.   61

Audrey. Do, good William.

William. God rest you merry, sir.   *Exit.*

Enter Corin.

Corin. Our master and mistress seeks you. Come away, away.   65

Touchstone. Trip, Audrey, trip, Audrey. I attend, I attend.   *Exeunt.*

SCENE 2

Enter Orlando and Oliver.

Orlando. Is't possible that on so little acquaintance you should like her? That, but seeing, you should love her? And loving, woo? And wooing, she should grant? And will you persever to enjoy her?   4

58 **bastinado** cudgel. **bandy** contend. 59 **faction** dissension. **o'errun** overwhelm. **policy** craft. 63 **God . . . merry** God keep you in good spirits. 4 **persever** persevere (stressed — ´ —).

Oliver. Neither call the giddiness of it in question, the poverty of her, the small acquaintance, my sudden wooing, nor sudden consenting. But say with me, 'I love Aliena'; say with her, that she loves me: consent with both, that we may enjoy each other. It shall be to your good: for my father's house and all the revenue that was old Sir Rowland's will I estate upon you, and here live and die a shepherd.

Enter Rosalind.

Orlando. You have my consent. Let your wedding be tomorrow; thither will I invite the Duke and all's contented followers. Go you and prepare Aliena for, look you, here comes my Rosalind. 16

Rosalind. God save you, brother.

Oliver. And you, fair sister. [*Exit.*]

Rosalind. O my dear Orlando, how it grieves me to see thee wear thy heart in a scarf. 20

Orlando. It is my arm.

Rosalind. I thought thy heart had been wounded with the claws of a lion.

Orlando. Wounded it is, but with the eyes of a lady.

Rosalind. Did your brother tell you how I counterfeited to sound when he show'd me your handkercher?

Orlando. Ay, and greater wonders than that. 27

Rosalind. O, I know where you are. Nay, 'tis true. There was never anything so sudden but the fight of two rams and Caesar's thrasonical brag of 'I came, saw, and overcame.' For your brother and my sister no sooner met, but they look'd; no sooner look'd, but they lov'd; no sooner lov'd, but they sigh'd; no

5 **giddiness** irresponsibility. 11 **estate** bestow. 14 **all's** all his. 20 **scarf** sling. 26 **sound** swoon. 28 **where you are** what you're getting at. 30 **thrasonical** boastful N.

sooner sigh'd, but they ask'd one another the reason;
no sooner knew the reason, but they sought the remedy. And in these degrees have they made a pair of
stairs to marriage, which they will climb incontinent,
or else be incontinent before marriage. They are in
the very wrath of love, and they will together. Clubs
cannot part them.   40

Orlando. They shall be married tomorrow, and I
will bid the Duke to the nuptial. But O, how bitter
a thing it is to look into happiness through another
man's eyes. By so much the more shall I tomorrow
be at the height of heart-heaviness, by how much I
shall think my brother happy in having what he
wishes for.

Rosalind. Why then, tomorrow I cannot serve your
turn for Rosalind?

Orlando. I can live no longer by thinking.   50

Rosalind. I will weary you then no longer with idle
talking. Know of me then—for now I speak to some
purpose—that I know you are a gentleman of good
conceit. I speak not this that you should bear a good
opinion of my knowledge, insomuch I say I know you
are. Neither do I labor for a greater esteem than
may in some little measure draw a belief from you,
to do yourself good and not to grace me. Believe
then, if you please, that I can do strange things. I
have, since I was three year old, convers'd with a
magician most profound in his art, and yet not damnable. If you do love Rosalind so near the heart as
your gesture cries it out, when your brother marries

36 **degrees** i.e. with a pun on *stairs*. 37 **incontinent** immediately.
38 **incontinent** unchaste. 54 **conceit** understanding. 58 **grace me**
do me honor. 60 **convers'd** associated. 61 **damnable** liable to
damnation because of magic practices. 63 **gesture** attitude.

Aliena shall you marry her. I know into what strait
of fortune she is driven, and it is not impossible t
me—if it appear not inconvenient to you—to set he
before your eyes tomorrow human as she is, and with
out any danger.

Orlando. Speak'st thou in sober meanings?   6

Rosalind. By my life, I do—which I tender dearly
though I say I am a magician. Therefore put you
in your best array, bid your friends; for if you wil
be married tomorrow, you shall, and to Rosalind, i
you will.   7

Enter Silvius and Phebe.

Look, here comes a lover of mine and a lover of hers

Phebe. Youth, you have done me much ungentlenes
To show the letter that I writ to you.

Rosalind. I care not if I have. It is my study
To seem despiteful and ungentle to you.
You are there followed by a faithful shepherd.   8
Look upon him, love him. He worships you.

Phebe. Good shepherd, tell this youth what 'tis t
love.

Silvius. It is to be all made of sighs and tears;
And so am I for Phebe.

Phebe. And I for Ganymede.   8

Orlando. And I for Rosalind.

Rosalind. And I for no woman.

Silvius. It is to be made of faith and service;
And so am I for Phebe.

Phebe. And I for Ganymede.   9

Orlando. And I for Rosalind.

Rosalind. And I for no woman.

67 **human** N. 70 **tender** value. 76 **ungentleness** discourtesy. 7
study endeavor. 79 **despiteful** mean.

Silvius. It is to be all made of fantasy,
All made of passion, and all made of wishes;
All adoration, duty, and observance;   95
All humbleness, all patience, and impatience;
All purity, all trial, all obedience;
And so am I for Phebe.
  Phebe. And so am I for Ganymede.
  Orlando. And so am I for Rosalind.   100
  Rosalind. And so am I for no woman.
  Phebe. [*To Rosalind.*] If this be so, why blame you
me to love you?
  Silvius. [*To Phebe.*] If this be so, why blame you
me to love you?   105
  Orlando. If this be so, why blame you me to love
you?
  Rosalind. Who do you speak to? 'Why blame you
me to love you?'   109
  Orlando. To her that is not here, nor doth not hear.
  Rosalind. Pray you, no more of this. 'Tis like the
howling of Irish wolves against the moon. [*To Silvius.*] I will help you if I can. [*To Phebe.*] I would
love you if I could. Tomorrow meet me all together.
[*To Phebe.*] I will marry you if ever I marry woman,
and I'll be married tomorrow. [*To Orlando.*] I will
satisfy you if ever I satisfied man, and you shall be
married tomorrow. [*To Silvius.*] I will content you
if what pleases you contents you, and you shall be
married tomorrow. As you love Rosalind, meet. As
you love Phebe, meet. And as I love no woman, I'll
meet. So fare you well. I have left you commands.
  Silvius. I'll not fail, if I live.

95 **observance** devotion. 97 **obedience** N. 103 **to love you for**
loving you. 108 **Who . . . you** N.

93

Phebe. Nor **I.**
Orlando. Nor **I.**   *Exeunt.*   125

SCENE 3

Enter Clown [Touchstone] and Audrey.

Touchstone. Tomorrow is the joyful day, Audrey.
Tomorrow will we be married.

Audrey. I do desire it with all my heart, and I hope
it is no dishonest desire to desire to be a woman of
the world. Here come two of the banish'd Duke's
pages.   6

Enter two Pages.

1 Page. Well met, honest gentleman.

Touchstone. By my troth, well met. Come, sit, sit—
and a song.

2 Page. We are for you. Sit i' th' middle.   10

1 Page. Shall we clap into 't roundly without hawk-
ing or spitting or saying we are hoarse, which are
the only prologues to a bad voice?

2 Page. I'faith, i'faith. And both in a tune, like two
gypsies on a horse.   15

Song

It was a lover and his lass,
    With a hey, and a ho, and a hey nonino,
That o'er the green cornfield did pass
    In the springtime, the only pretty ring time,
When birds do sing, hey ding a ding, ding.   20
Sweet lovers love the spring.

4 **dishonest** immodest. **woman of the world** married woman.
10 **We are for you** we agree with you. 11 **clap into't roundly**
start briskly. 14 **in a tune** in unison. 16 **Song** N. 19 **ring time**
wedding time.
   94

Between the acres of the rye,
    With a hey, and a ho, and a hey nonino,
These pretty country folks would lie
    In springtime, etc.   25

This carol they began that hour,
    With a hey, and a ho, and a hey nonino,
How that life was but a flower
    In springtime, etc.

And therefore take the present time,   30
    With a hey, and a ho, and a hey nonino,
For love is crowned with the prime
    In springtime, etc.

Touchstone. Truly, young gentlemen, though there
were no great matter in the ditty, yet the note was
very untuneable.   36

1 Page. You are deceiv'd, sir. We kept time; we lost
not our time.

Touchstone. By my troth, yes. I count it but time
lost to hear such a foolish song. God buy you, and
God mend your voices. Come, Audrey.   *Exeunt.* 41

SCENE 4

Enter Duke Senior, Amiens, Jaques, Orlando,
        Oliver, Celia.

Duke Senior. Dost thou believe, Orlando, that the
    boy
Can do all this that he hath promised?

Orlando. I sometimes do believe and sometimes do
    not,
As those that fear they hope and know they fear.

22 **Between . . . acres** on the strips between acres. 26 **carol** N.
35 **note** tune. 36 **untuneable** discordant. 40 **buy** be with. 4 **As . . .
fear** N.

Enter Rosalind, Silvius, and Phebe.

Rosalind. Patience once more whiles our compact is
urg'd.   5
You say, if I bring in your Rosalind,
You will bestow her on Orlando here?
Duke Senior. That would I, had I kingdoms to give
with her.
Rosalind. And you say that you will have her when
I bring her?   9
Orlando. That would I, were I of all kingdoms king.
Rosalind. You say you'll marry me, if I be willing?
Phebe. That will I, should I die the hour after.
Rosalind. But if you do refuse to marry me,
You'll give yourself to this most faithful shepherd?
Phebe. So is the bargain.   15
Rosalind. You say that you'll have Phebe, if she
will?
Silvius. Though to have her and death were both
one thing.
Rosalind. I have promis'd to make all this matter
even.
Keep you your word, O Duke, to give your daughter;
You yours, Orlando, to receive his daughter;   20
Keep you your word, Phebe, that you'll marry me
Or else, refusing me, to wed this shepherd;
Keep your word, Silvius, that you'll marry her
If she refuse me. And from hence I go
To make these doubts all even.   25
                                    Exeunt Rosalind and Celia.
Duke Senior. I do remember in this shepherd boy

5 **whiles** while. **compact** agreement (stressed — ́). **urg'd**
pressed forward, expedited. 18 **I have** to be read 'I've.' 25 **doubts**
impossibilities. **even** plain.

Some lively touches of my daughter's favor.

Orlando. My lord, the first time that I e'er saw him
Methought he was a brother to your daughter.
But, my good lord, this boy is forest born   30
And hath been tutor'd in the rudiments
Of many desperate studies by his uncle,
Whom he reports to be a great magician

Enter Clown [Touchstone] and Audrey.

Obscured in the circle of this forest.   34

Jaques. There is sure another flood toward, and
these couples are coming to the ark. Here comes a
pair of very strange beasts, which in all tongues are
call'd fools.

Touchstone. Salutation and greeting to you all.   39

Jaques. Good my lord, bid him welcome. This is the
motley—minded gentleman that I have so often met in
the forest. He hath been a courtier, he swears.

Touchstone. If any man doubt that, let him put me
to my purgation. I have trod a measure; I have
flatt'red a lady; I have been politic with my friend,
smooth with mine enemy; I have undone three tailors;
I have had four quarrels, and like to have fought
one.

Jaques. And how was that tane up?   49

Touchstone. Faith, we met and found the quarrel
was upon the seventh cause.

Jaques. How 'seventh cause'? Good my lord, like
this fellow.

Duke Senior. I like him very well.   54

27 **lively** lifelike. **touches** traces. **favor** appearance. 28 **e'er** F *ever*.
32 **desperate** dangerous because they deal with forbidden arts.
34 **Obscured** hidden. 35 **toward** about to occur. 44 **purgation**
proof. **measure** a stately dance. 46 **three tailors** N. 47 **like** . . .
fought came near fighting. 49 **tane up** made up.

Touchstone. God 'ild you, sir; I desire you of the like. I press in here, sir, amongst the rest of the country copulatives to swear and to forswear, according as marriage binds and blood breaks. A poor virgin, sir, an ill-favor'd thing, sir, but mine own. A poor humor of mine, sir, to take that that no man else will. Rich honesty dwells like a miser, sir, in a poor house, as your pearl in your foul oyster.

Duke Senior. By my faith, he is very swift and sententious.   64

Touchstone. According to the fool's bolt, sir, and such dulcet diseases.

Jaques. But for the seventh cause. How did you find the quarrel on the seventh cause?

Touchstone. Upon a lie seven times removed—bear your body more seeming, Audrey—as thus, sir: I did dislike the cut of a certain courtier's beard. He sent me word, if I said his beard was not cut well, he was in the mind it was. This is call'd the Retort Courteous. If I sent him word again it was not well cut, he would send me word he cut it to please himself. This is call'd the Quip Modest. If again, it was not well cut, he disabled my judgment. This is called the Reply Churlish. If again, it was not well cut, he would answer I spake not true. This is call'd the Reproof Valiant. If again, it was not well cut, he would say I lie. This is call'd the Countercheck Quar-

55 God'ild God reward. 57 copulatives those about to be married. 58 blood passion. 60 humor whim. 61 honesty chastity. 63 sententious pithy. 65 fool's bolt N. 66 dulcet diseases N. 70 seeming becomingly. 71 dislike indicate disapproval of. 76 Quip retort. 77 disabled disparaged. 81 Countercheck rebuff (a term from chess).

relsome. And so to the Lie Circumstantial and the Lie Direct.

Jaques. And how oft did you say his beard was not well cut? 85

Touchstone. I durst go no further than the Lie Circumstantial, nor he durst not give me the Lie Direct. And so we measur'd swords and parted.

Jaques. Can you nominate in order now the degrees of the lie? 90

Touchstone. O sir, we quarrel in print, by the book, as you have books for good manners. I will name you the degrees: the first, the Retort Courteous; the second, the Quip Modest; the third, the Reply Churlish; the fourth, the Reproof Valiant; the fift, the Countercheck Quarrelsome; the sixt, the Lie with Circumstance; the seventh, the Lie Direct. All these you may avoid but the Lie Direct, and you may avoid that too, with an If. I knew when seven justices could not take up a quarrel, but when the parties were met themselves, one of them thought but of an If—as, 'If you said so, then I said so,' and they shook hands and swore brothers. Your If is the only peacemaker. Much virtue in If. 104

Jaques. Is not this a rare fellow, my lord? He's as good at anything, and yet a fool.

Duke Senior. He uses his folly like a stalking horse, and under the presentation of that he shoots his wit.

---

82 the (before *Lie Circumstantial*) F omits. 88 measur'd i.e. before dueling. 89 nominate name. 91 book N. 95 fift fifth. 96 sixt sixth. 103 swore brothers made a blood pact. 107 stalking horse decoy N. 108 presentation semblance.

Enter Hymen, Rosalind, and Celia.

Still Music.

Hymen. Then is there mirth in heaven
 When earthly things made even   110
  Atone together.
 Good Duke, receive thy daughter;
 Hymen from heaven brought her,
  Yea, brought her hether,
 That thou mightst join her hand with his 115
 Whose heart within his bosom is.

Rosalind. To you I give myself, for I am yours. [*To Duke.*]

To you I give myself, for I am yours. [*To Orlando.*]

 Duke Senior. If there be truth in sight, you are my daughter.

 Orlando. If there be truth in sight, you are my Rosalind. 120

 Phebe. If sight and shape be true,

Why then, my love adieu.

 Rosalind. I'll have no father, if you be not he.

I'll have no husband, if you be not he.

Nor ne'er wed woman, if you be not she. 125

 Hymen. Peace ho! I bar confusion.

'Tis I must make conclusion

 Of these most strange events.

Here's eight that must take hands

To join in Hymen's bands, 130

 If truth holds true contents.

You and you no cross shall part. [*To Orland and Rosalind.*]

You and you are heart in heart. [*To Oliver and Celia.*]

SD Still **Music** soft music. 109 **Hymen** the Greek and Roman god of marriage. 111 **Atone** unite. 131 **truth** . . . **contents** i.e. if the truth be the truth.

You to his love must accord,
Or have a woman to your lord. [*To Phebe.*]   135
You and you are sure together
As the winter to foul weather. [*To Touchstone and
    Audrey.*]
Whiles a wedlock hymn we sing,
Feed yourselves with questioning,
That reason wonder may diminish   140
How thus we met and these things finish.

Song

Wedding is great Juno's crown:
    O blessed bond of board and bed!
'Tis Hymen peoples every town.
    High wedlock then be honored: 145
Honor, high honor, and renown
To Hymen, God of every town.

Duke Senior. O my dear niece, welcome thou art to
me,
E'en daughter, welcome, in no less degree.   149
    Phebe. I will not eat my word; now thou art mine.
Thy faith my fancy to thee doth combine. [*To Silvius.*]

Enter Second Brother [*Jaques de Boys*].

Second Brother. Let me have audience for a word
or two.
I am the second son of old Sir Rowland
That brings these tidings to this fair assembly.
Duke Frederick, hearing how that every day   155
Men of great worth resorted to this forest,
Address'd a mighty power which were on foot

136 **sure together** permanently bound together. 140 **reason** explanation. 142 **Juno's** N. 145 **High** solemn. 149 **E'en** F *Even.*
157 **Address'd** prepared. **power** force.

In his own conduct, purposely to take
His brother here and put him to the sword.
And to the skirts of this wild wood he came,   160
Where, meeting with an old religious man,
After some question with him was converted
Both from his enterprise and from the world,
His crown bequeathing to his banish'd brother
And all their lands restor'd to them again   165
That were with him exil'd. This to be true
I do engage my life.
  Duke Senior.   Welcome, young man.
Thou offer'st fairly to thy brothers' wedding:
To one his lands witheld, and to the other
A land itself at large, a potent dukedom.   170
First, in this forest let us do those ends
That here were well begun and well begot.
And after, every of this happy number
That have endur'd shrewd days and nights with us
Shall share the good of our returned fortune,   175
According to the measure of their states.
Meantime forget this new-falne dignity
And fall into our rustic revelry.
Play, music, and you brides and bridegrooms all,
With measure heap'd in joy, to th' measures fall.   180
  Jaques. Sir, by your patience. If I heard you
    rightly,
The Duke hath put on a religious life

158 **In his own conduct** under his leadership. 161 **religious man**
hermit. 162 **question** conversation. 166 **exil'd** stressed — ´.
167 **engage** pledge. 168 **offer'st fairly** give most generously. 170
potent powerful. 171 **do those ends** complete those purposes. 173
every every one. 174 **shrewd** severe, difficult. 177 **new-falne**
recently acquired. 180 **measure** due proportion. **measures** dances.
181 **by your patience** by your leave.

And thrown into neglect the pompous court.
Second Brother. He hath.
Jaques. To him will I. Out of these convertites   185
There is much matter to be heard and learn'd.
You to your former honor I bequeath; [*To Duke.*]
Your patience and your virtue well deserves it.
You to a love that your true faith doth merit. [*To
    Orlando.*]
You to your land and love and great allies. [*To
    Oliver.*]   190
You to a long and well-deserved bed. [*To Silvius.*]
And you to wrangling, for thy loving voyage [*To
    Touchstone.*]
Is but for two months victuall'd. So to your pleas-
    ures.
I am for other than for dancing measures.
Duke Senior. Stay, Jaques, stay.   195
Jaques. To see no pastime I. What you would have
I'll stay to know at your abandon'd cave.   *Exit.*
Duke Senior. Proceed, proceed. We will begin these
    rites,
As we do trust they'll end, in true delights.   *Exit.*

[*Epilogue*]

*Rosalind. It is not the fashion to see the lady the
epilogue, but it is no more unhandsome than to see
the lord the prologue. If it be true that good wine
needs no bush, 'tis true that a good play needs no
epilogue. Yet to good wine they do use good bushes,*

183 **pompous** ceremonious. 185 **convertites** converts. 2 **unhand-**
some improper. 3 **wine** . . . **bush** N.

and good plays prove the better by the help of good epilogues. What a case am I in then, that am neither a good epilogue nor cannot insinuate with you in the behalf of a good play. I am not furnish'd like a beggar; therefore to beg will not become me. My way is to conjure you, and I'll begin with the women. I charge you, O women, for the love you bear to men, to like as much of this play as please you. And I charge you, O men, for the love you bear to women —as I perceive by your simp'ring none of you hates them—that between you and the women the play may please. If I were a woman, I would kiss as many of you as had beards that pleas'd me, complexions that lik'd me, and breaths that I defied not. And I am sure as many as have good beards or good faces or sweet breaths will for my kind offer, when I make curtsy, bid me farewell. Exit.

Finis

8 insinuate ingratiate myself. 17 woman N. 19 defied disliked. 22 bid me farewell i.e. a plea for applause.

NOTES

Act I, Scene 1

2 he This word is omitted in the Folio. Though this sentence may be understood without the addition of *he*, the sense is clarified with its inclusion. Folio omissions of this sort will be noted hereafter at the foot of the page. Square brackets around stage directions indicate material not found in the Folio but necessary to explain the action.

32 mar The bantering conjunction of *make* and *mar* is common. For example, see *Love's Labour's Lost*, IV.3.190–2.

39 prodigal portion A reference to the biblical story of the prodigal son (Luke 15).

52 reverence That is, 'The fact that you are older puts you closer to that reverence associated with the head of the family.' Oliver bridles at Orlando's ironic compliment, as his next words indicate.

56 villain Oliver uses this word in the modern sense of 'an evil person,' while Orlando's interpretation of the word conforms to its original meaning: 'a person of low birth, a servant.' At this stage in the action Orlando has seized his brother.

90 wrastler This Folio spelling indicates a common Elizabethan pronunciation. Hereafter words of this kind will appear at the foot of the page: **wrastler** wrestler.

97 Monsieur Spelled *Mounsieur* in the Folio at this point, but elsewhere regularly *Monsieur*.

114 Forest of Arden Certainly Shakespeare derived this name from Lodge's novel, *Rosalynde* (see Appendix B), but in addition to the Forest of the Ardennes in France there is a Forest of Arden in Warwickshire. The appearance of palm trees and lions, incongruous in either locale, is explained once we see Shakespeare's forest as an imaginary Arcadia. Arden was also his mother's maiden name.

118 golden world The Golden Age of classical mythology, like the Garden of Eden, was characterized by happiness and innocence.

Act I, Scene 2

32 housewife Fortune The standard symbol of Fortune is, of course, the wheel—an image characteristic of the medieval and Elizabethan world. For example, Fluellen speaks of Fortune being 'painted also with a wheel, to signify to you, which is the moral of it, that she is turning, and inconstant, and mutability, and variation' (*Henry V*, III.6.33). In the present passage Celia is reducing Fortune to the status of a housewife with her spinning wheel.

43 Nature The antithesis between Nature and Fortune in this and the following lines is a characteristic Elizabethan concern. The idea is that Nature is the powerful creator and includes Fortune. Thus Nature cannot be guided by Fortune.

55 whetstone Though we do not learn the Clown's name until later in the play, the pun on *Touchstone* is obvious here. A clown is, of course, the court fool or jester.

84 Celia In the Folio this speech is assigned incorrectly to Rosalind, which would cause both of the dukes to have the same first name.

85 enough This is the Folio reading. An alternate reading could be: 'My father's love is enough to honor him. Enough!'

98 Bon jour The Folio spelling *Boon-iour* (*i* pronounced *j*) is perhaps indicative of common Elizabethan pronunciation of French.

108 smell A pun on the two meanings of *rank*: 'position' and 'odor.'

120 old tale Celia means that there is nothing novel or unusual about Le Beau's introduction.

125 presents A legal phrase meaning 'by this present document' and with a pun on 'presence.'

127 which The construction here is archaic: 'which . . . him' equals 'whom' and 'which . . . his' equals 'whose.'

143 broken music That is, to hear the music of having his ribs broken. Broken music is technically 'part music,' or music performed by instruments of different classes. The term could also refer to a musical instrument with its 'ribs' broken.

161 such . . . man The man is of course Charles, the wrestler of greater strength, and the meaning is clearly that the odds are all on his side.

165 hether The Folio spelling *hether* indicates a common Elizabethan pronunciation, though the word as it appears throughout the Folio is most often spelled in the modern fashion.

169 them Here used as a term of respect to include both Rosalind and Celia.

249 out of suits The meaning here is twofold: Rosalind means that she is no longer in Fortune's service (wearing Fortune's livery) and that her suits are rejected by Fortune.

254 quintain Used for jousting practice, this was an upright post with the figure of an armed man attached to it on a horizontal bar. The object was to ride full tilt against it and avoid being struck by the figure as it swung about.

269 humorous The Duke is temperamental in the sense of a Jonsonian 'humour' character. He is ruled by one guiding passion, in this case obstinacy.

275 taller Many editors have emended this to 'smaller' in order to eliminate Shakespeare's obvious inconsistency here, for Rosalind is later described as being taller than Celia (I.3.114).

Act I, Scene 3

SD Rosalind The Folio reads *Rosaline* at this point and elsewhere either *Rosalind* or *Rosalinde*.

8 reasons A particularly indelicate pun is suggested by the similarity in Elizabethan pronunciation between 'reason' and 'raising.' See Helge Kökeritz, *Shakespeare's Pronunciation* (New Haven, 1953), pp. 138–9.

19 'hem' . . . him A play on the similarity in pronunciation of these two words.

36 deserve well That is, to be hated—though Rosalind interprets the remark in an opposite fashion. Celia, in using the word containing 'serve,' is playing on the similarity in pronunciation of 'hate' and 'eat.'

74 Juno's swans The swan was traditionally sacred to Venus, the peacock to Juno. But Professor J. R. Crawford has pointed out a similar reference in Thomas Kyd's *Soliman and Perseda* (IV.1.70).

101 **change** That is, of fortune. This has sometimes been emended to *charge*, the reading of the Second Folio. But here *change*, in the sense of reversal of fortune, makes intelligible sense.

124 **Ganymede** A handsome boy whom Zeus made cupbearer of the gods. The name is spelled *Ganimed* in the Folio.

Act II, Scene 1

3 **painted** The contrast between country life and court life was a characteristic theme in Elizabethan literature. The court, with its artificiality and hypocrisy, was compared unfavorably to the natural grace of the country. The Forest of Arden is just such a natural and idyllic place as this, far from the pomp of the court.

5 **the penalty of Adam** The change of seasons is, of course, the penalty of Adam after his loss of Paradise. The *not* in this line has been often unnecessarily emended to 'but.' However, the Folio reading of *not* is consistent when we realize that the Duke is merely asking another rhetorical question.

13 **toad** It was an ancient superstition that the jewel called the 'toadstone' was to be found in the head of the toad.

18 **Amiens** Most editors assign the first five words of Amiens' speech to the Duke. But there is no occasion to depart from the Folio reading and no reason to assume that Amiens would not immediately agree with the Duke and say: 'I would not change it.'

26 **Jaques** Not to be confused with Orlando's youngest brother, Jaques de Boys, who appears briefly in the last act. Scansion obviously indicates the name is to be pronounced as dissyllabic here; in Elizabethan speech its *qu* was sounded *k*: 'Jā-kes.'

49 **there** This word appears only in the First Folio and is omitted in the others. Its inclusion makes a six-foot line, but this is not an uncommon method of varying the blank verse pattern.

50 **velvet** In other words, with the velvet on their horns they are like courtiers wearing velvet clothes.

Act II, Scene 3

SD **Enter . . . Adam** It is obvious here that Adam and Orlando enter from opposite sides of the stage.

108

Act II, Scene 4

1 weary The Folio reading is *merry* but Theobald's emendation is obviously necessary. In Shakespeare's writing 'wery' and 'mery' could easily be confused.

12 cross The pun here develops from an alternate meaning of the word. Old pennies had crosses stamped on one side.

16 Arden The pun here develops from the similarity in pronunciation between 'Arden' and 'harden.' Harden was a coarse fabric made from flax or hemp and was the term used to describe the smock worn by country laborers. See Helge Kökeritz, *Shakespeare's Pronunciation* (New Haven, 1953), p. 91. The idea is further elaborated in line 18 where *travelers* gives an echo of 'travail' or 'labor.' Jaques means that he has now become a complete rustic.

55 mortal The word is used in two slightly different ways in this sentence: as 'subject to death' and as 'humanly foolish.'

67 kinsman Rosalind is here playing on the two meanings of *clown*—'jester' and 'peasant.'

Act II, Scene 5

54 Ducdame Many attempts have been made to ascertain the meaning of this word. Hanmer's reading 'duc ad me' is conceivable, as is Dover Wilson's belief that it is derived from a corruption of the Romani 'dukrá mē' (I foretell). This latter explanation would enrich the idea that the Duke and his followers are living as gypsies and would explain the reference to Egypt, the supposed home of the gypsies. But there is no satisfactory explanation, and certainly Jaques would think these conjectures merely a further illustration of the folly of the world.

60 circle The ancient superstitious belief was that spirits could be conjured up in this fashion.

61 first born of Egypt Perhaps Jaques is railing against those of high degree, particularly the two Dukes, or he may be making a comment on the gypsy life in the Forest of Arden (the conjecture advanced by Dover Wilson).

Act II, Scene 7

6 discord . . . spheres Ptolemy's astronomical system maintained that the spheres revolving about the earth produced a harmonious melody. The Duke is elaborating on the incongruity of Jaques producing anything melodious.

13 **motley** Common stage tradition has always regarded this as the checkered costume of the court jester. Leslie Hotson, in *Shakespeare's Motley* (Oxford, 1952), considers this an anachronistic picture. He advances the theory that Elizabethan stage fools wore a long gown made of motley—a subdued cloth mixture like homespun or tweed.

26 **hour** This passage is particularly rich in indelicate puns. The basic pattern is established when we realize the identity in Elizabethan pronunciation between 'hour' and 'whore,' leading to Touchstone's play on the word *tale* in l. 28.

26 **ripe** The first meaning here is 'grow ripe,' but the additional meaning of 'search' fits well with the puns established in the preceding note.

30 **Chanticleer** The cock, seen also in *Reynard the Fox* and Chaucer's *Nun's Priest's Tale*.

44 **suit** A play on the two meanings of the word, 'request' and 'clothing' (which continues with *weed* in l. 45).

73 **weary very means** The phrase is obviously corrupt and there is very little satisfactory explanation. Wright's emendation of *weary* to *wearer's* furthers the idea of the extravagant amount spent on clothes. Dover Wilson would emend *means* to *mints*, thus enlarging the idea of national bankruptcy. Perhaps a more reasonable solution lies in the fact that 'means' and 'mains' were pronounced in the same fashion, 'main' being the high sea. In general, the sense is that pride (extravagance in dress) flows in huge quantity like the sea, until finally the very source becomes dried up.

100 **reason** The identity in Elizabethan pronunciation between 'reason' and 'raisin' explains the pun here. The banquet consisted of sweetmeats and fruit such as grapes (raisins).

158 **pantaloon** The stock figure of a foolish old man in the Italian *commedia dell'arte*.

Act III, Scene 1

6 **candle** The reference here is to Luke 15:8.

Act III, Scene 2

2 **Queen of Night** The Queen is 'thrice crowned' in her capacity as Proserpina, Luna, and Diana.

4 huntress' name Rosalind, as a young maiden, owed homage to Diana, goddess of the hunt.

41 manners The word is used here in the two senses of 'etiquette' and 'morality.'

61 tarr'd Tar was regularly used by shepherds to salve sore spots on their animals.

82 cuckoldly The cuckold, or betrayed husband, was traditionally described as wearing horns.

88 Ind The Folio spelling of the rhyme words in this passage indicates the forced rhyme of the poem—*Inde:Rosalinde: winde: Rosalinde: Linde:Rosalinde: mind:Rosalinde*, etc.

98 butter-women's rank In other words, the verses jog along like a crowd of women riding to market to sell their butter.

108 to cart On their way to jail loose women were driven through the streets in a cart. Touchstone is also using the word in the sense of putting the harvest in a wagon.

119 medlar A small brown-skinned apple, eaten only when decayed. There is a pun, of course, on 'meddler.'

157 Jupiter Most editors follow Spedding's emendation of *Jupiter* to *pulpiter* to conform to the idea of preaching in the rest of the sentence. However, as merely representing a mild oath, the Folio reading is equally acceptable.

179 Pythagoras' time The reference here is to Pythagoras' doctrine of the transmigration of souls.

180 Irish rat This refers to the old belief that Irish magicians could kill animals with rhymed spells.

197 Good my complexion Rosalind appeals to her woman's nature not to cause her to blush.

200 South Sea of discovery In other words, Rosalind is saying that further delay will seem as long as a voyage of discovery to the South Seas.

228 Gargantua's mouth Originally this was the name of a giant in French folklore, a legend later used by Rabelais whose giant Gargantua swallows five pilgrims in a salad.

239 Jove's tree The oak was sacred to Jove (Jupiter).

274 goldsmiths' wives . . . rings Jaques is saying that Orlando is so revoltingly poetical that he must have learned the mottoes on rings sold by goldsmiths' wives. These rings were love tokens and had romantic sentiments engraved on the inside.

276 **painted cloth** Cheap cloth was often painted with scenes and mottoes in imitation of tapestry. Orlando is saying that Jaques has learned just as many platitudes from this source.

279 **Atalanta's heels** Atalanta, renowned for her swiftness, forced suitors to compete with her in a foot race.

401 **dark house** The whip and the dark room represented the extent of Elizabethan treatment of the insane. For example, compare with the treatment of Malvolio in *Twelfth Night*.

422 **liver** In ancient medicine the liver was believed to be the seat of love.

Act III, Scene 3

3 **feature** It is obvious from Audrey's answer that she has not understood Touchstone's remark. The words 'fetter,' 'faitour' (a cheat), and 'feature' were pronounced in an identical fashion in Elizabethan English, and it is difficult to know exactly what word Audrey had in mind.

7 **capricious** This word is derived from the Latin *caper* meaning a 'he-goat,' thus strengthening Touchstone's pun.

8 **Goths** The identical pronunciation of 'goats' and 'Goths' (where the *th* is sounded *t*) in Elizabethan English explains this pun.

14 **reckoning . . . room** That is, an excessive bill for poor accommodations. Many editors have seen in this line a reference to Marlowe's death on May 30, 1593, in a quarrel over a tavern bill, finding in addition an echo of his line in the *Jew of Malta*: 'infinite riches in a little room' (I.1.37). But Marlowe's death occurred six years before the date of *As You Like It*, and it seems doubtful that Shakespeare is making a conscious reference here, though Dover Wilson has advanced the hypothesis that a first draft of the play was composed in 1593 (see Appendix A).

42 **Sir** This was the title of a bachelor of a university (*Dominus*). But the title was used loosely and was the usual form of address for a priest.

48 **heart** The pun on 'hart' is strengthened by 'stag' (*stagger*) and *horn-beasts* in the next line.

49 **horn-beasts** Here again is the common Elizabethan symbol for the cuckold or deceived husband.

112

70 **Master What-ye-call't** In Elizabethan English Jaques' name normally sounded the same as 'jakes' meaning 'privy.' Touchstone's humorous fastidiousness is revealed when he refuses to pronounce the word.

96 **O sweet Oliver** Though this is printed as prose in the Folio, Touchstone is singing bits of an old ballad, licensed in 1584.

Act III, Scene 4

7 **dissembling color** Judas, the betrayer of Christ, is portrayed as having red hair, the traditional sign of the untrustworthy.

41 **traverse athwart** In other words, like an unskillful jouster who breaks his lance by hitting his opponent's shield on an angle.

52 **pale complexion** The sighs of the true lover were supposed to draw blood from the heart and cause paleness.

Act III, Scene 5

39 **candle . . . bed** Rosalind is saying that Phebe lacks Beauty's blaze—that is, her beauty is not bright enough to light her to bed without a candle.

50 **south** In England a south wind brings fog and rain.

62 **Foul . . . scoffer** *Foul* is used here with two meanings: 'ugly' and 'evil.' In other words, Rosalind is saying that Phebe is doubly foul, being both ugly and a scoffer.

80 **Dead shepherd** Another reference to Marlowe. The maxim is from his *Hero and Leander* (i.176) published in 1598. But there is little reason to assume that this reference changes the date of the play (see Appendix A).

90 **neighborly** Phebe is making a distinction between love and friendship.

108 **Carlot** Used here as a proper name, as the italics in the Folio clearly indicate. As a noun the word means 'peasant' or 'churl.'

133 **omittance . . . quittance** A proverb meaning 'to refrain from paying is not to discharge a debt.'

Act IV, Scene 1

58 **horns** A further reference to the cuckold.

85 **suit** Rosalind continues her play on words with *apparel* in the next line.

113

96 Troilus This famous lover of Cressida was killed, not ingloriously by a club, but by the spear of Achilles.

99 Leander Hero and Leander were the classical prototypes of great lovers. Each night Leander swam the Hellespont to visit Hero in Sestos. For her purpose Rosalind chooses to regard them in mock heroic terms.

152 Diana The figure of Diana was common in garden statuary. There is no reason to suppose that any particular statue is being referred to here.

164 'Wit . . . wilt?' A proverbial phrase indicating that the person's intelligence is deserting him. It is also roughly equivalent to 'Hold your tongue.'

172 occasion In other words, a woman must be able to use her fault to advantage and turn the blame on her husband.

202 bird . . . nest Compare to the proverb: 'It is a foul bird defiles its own nest.'

210 bastard of Venus According to myth Cupid was the child of Venus, goddess of love, and Mars, god of war.

Act IV, Scene 2

12 The rest . . . burthen Most editors have assumed that 'The rest shall bear this burthen' was a stage direction referring to the refrain following, even though the phrase is printed in the First Folio in italics as part of the song. Dover Wilson was the first to point out that the Folio reading could be justified.

Act IV, Scene 3

18 Phoenix A miraculous bird fabled to live in Arabia. It was supposed to live for five hundred years and then be reborn from its own ashes.

34 Turk In other words, Phebe is being as barbarous as the infidel Turks in their attacks upon Christians. This refers to the time of the Crusades.

Act V, Scene 2

30 thrasonical Thraso, the braggart soldier in Terence's *Eunuchus*, was the prototype of the boaster.

114

67 human In other words, Rosalind will actually appear and will not be a phantom summoned by incantation.

97 obedience In the Folio *observance* is repeated here, and it is logical to assume that this was a printer's error and follow Malone's emendation.

108 Who . . . you The Folio reading 'Why do you speak too, Why blame you me to love you' is understandable but makes Orlando's answer somewhat awkward, so Rowe's emendation is followed here.

Act V, Scene 3

16 Song The fourth stanza appears as the second in the Folio, but the text of the Edinburgh MS seems more logical.

26 carol This word is not used in the specialized modern sense but refers to any song at a festival. It originally meant a 'ring dance.'

Act V, Scene 4

4 As . . . fear This is a difficult line to interpret. The meaning may be: 'like those who are afraid they are really only dreaming and at the same time are fully aware of the logic of their fear.'

46 three tailors Touchstone means that his extravagance in dress and failure to pay his bills had ruined three merchants.

65 fool's bolt A *bolt* is literally a blunt arrow. The old proverb runs: 'A fool's bolt is soon spent.'

66 dulcet diseases 'Pleasant ailments.' In other words, to listen to a fool is an enjoyable experience.

91 book Touchstone is satirizing the many books on swordsmanship and good manners popular in Elizabethan England. There is, for example, Castiglione's *Il Cortegiano*, translated in 1561.

107 stalking horse A real or artificial horse under cover of which a hunter approached his game.

142 Juno's Juno was the queen of the gods and the symbol of married virtue.

115

Epilogue

3 wine . . . bush This is an ancient proverb derived from the
fact that an ivy bush was the sign of a vintner's shop. Rosalind
means that good wine needs no advertisement.

17 woman On the Elizabethan stage women's parts were of
course taken by young boys.

APPENDIX A

Text and Date

As You Like It was not printed until the First Folio of 1623. As this is the only authoritative text, it has been the concern of the present edition to depart from the Folio reading only when absolutely necessary. Essential stage directions not found in the Folio have been placed in square brackets, while words added to the text have been noted at the foot of the page. Obvious errors have been silently corrected and the spelling has been modernized (as has the punctuation) except in the case of a spelling indicative of Elizabethan pronunciation.

However, the question of the date of the play's composition presents significant difficulties. The play was entered on the Stationer's Register as a book to be stayed (that is, not printed, in order to prevent unauthorized use of the text) on August 4 of an unspecified year. But the order of entries in the Register and the inclusion of *Henry V*, *Much Ado about Nothing*, and Jonson's *Every Man in his Humour* on the same list make it almost certain that it was the year 1600. This information, however, tells us little about the time of actual composition.

John Dover Wilson, in *The New Shakespeare* (Cambridge, 1926), advances the hypothesis that a first version of the play was written in the summer of 1593 and drastically revised to its present form sometime around 1600. His argument is based upon a number of interesting points of internal evidence: the existence of many blank-verse lines in prose passages of the text as we now have it, the presence of obvious inconsistencies (Celia being 'taller' than Rosalind), certain references to the Martin Marprelate controversy, the publication of Lodge's *Rosalynde* in 1590, and most significant of all, the overt references to Christopher Marlowe.

At one point in the play Touchstone mentions a man being struck more dead than 'a great reckoning in a little room.' Dover Wilson feels that this is a direct reference to Marlowe's death in a tavern brawl on May 30, 1593, with the additional echo of a line from the *Jew of Malta* (see note to *As You Like It*, III.3.14). Marlowe is again referred to in III.5.81, where his *Hero and Leander*, published in 1598, is quoted. A topical allusion of this sort would suggest that Shakespeare wrote the play some time after the year 1598. But Touchstone's remark must be taken as particularly inconclusive evidence that the play was first written in 1593. At best it can be interpreted only as an unconscious reference on Shakespeare's part and, if conscious, talk about Marlowe's death must have been common for many years after 1593. Even as late as 1600 a London audience could be assumed to have understood the allusion. However, it is most significant that Francis Meres in his discussion of Shakespeare's plays, published in 1598, makes no mention of *As You Like It*.

Though Dover Wilson's theory is of great interest and ingeniously conceived, internal and external evidence seem to point most clearly to a date of composition sometime between 1598 and 1600. Until further evidence is disclosed it is impossible to be more definite. Certainly the first mention of the play occurs in 1600.

APPENDIX B

Source

'or *As You Like It* Shakespeare characteristically derived his
basic plot from another author. In this case all essential material
comes from Thomas Lodge's novel, *Rosalynde: Euphues Golden
Legacie*, published in 1590. In a note to his 'gentlemen readers'
Lodge remarks, 'If you like it, so'—and it is generally assumed
that this gave rise to Shakespeare's title. Shakespeare has abandoned the mannered euphuistic style of his source but has re-
tained many of the pastoral elements which can be seen in his
idyllic Forest of Arden, far away from the artificiality of court
life. This popular Elizabethan theme can be found in a multi-
tude of other words, among them Spenser's *Shepheardes Calender*
1579) and Sidney's *Arcadia* (1590).

Lodge's novel (in turn based on a Middle English poem, *The
Coke's Tale of Gamelyn*) is a traditional pastoral romance.
Shakespeare, while changing some names, has followed the
essential pattern of Lodge's narrative. Rosalynde is the daughter of the banished king of France who falls in love with Rosader
(Orlando) when she sees him in a wrestling match. She and her
cousin Alinda (Celia) are banished by the usurping king and go
in the disguises of Ganymede and Aliena to the Forest of the
Ardennes. Here they meet Rosader who has fled from the wrath
of his wicked brother Saladyne (Oliver). There is a romance
between Rosalynde and Rosader, as in Shakespeare's play; and
Saladyne, himself exiled by the evil king, reforms and falls in
love with Alinda. News is finally brought to the forest that the
peers of France have risen against the usurper, who is defeated,
and Rosader is made heir to the throne.

It is obvious that *As You Like It* owes much to Lodge's novel,
but Shakespeare has made some significant changes and additions. He has focused the action most clearly on the Forest of
Arden passages, cutting out a great deal of the introductory
matter, particularly the long section on Rosader's quarrel with
his wicked brother, which he compressed to one brief interview.

He also concentrated upon the romance of Rosalynde and Rosader and, unlike Lodge, gave merely a brief account of Saladyne's love for Alinda. But changes of this sort are obviously necessitated by the transition from a narrative to a dramatic form and reflect little of Shakespeare's originality.

The significant difference between *As You Like It* and *Rosalynde* lies in the approach to the pastoral tradition. The characters that Shakespeare has added—Touchstone, Jaques, and Audrey—create a tone of realism and form an ironic double image commenting upon the stilted world of pastoral romance. Perhaps more important even than the treatment of these three characters is Shakespeare's treatment of Rosalind: she is no longer the stock figure that Lodge's Rosalynde was, and the whole action of the play is centered sharply on her, thus eliminating the diffusion characteristic of the novel. She has become a witty, paradoxical young lady, a blend of realism and of romance—fit company for Orlando and fit company too for Touchstone and Jaques.

APPENDIX C

Reading List

OSCAR JAMES CAMPBELL, *Shakespeare's Satire*, New York, 1943, pp. 44–64.

H. B. CHARLTON, *Shakespearian Comedy*, London, 1938, pp. 277–97.

CUMBERLAND CLARK, *A Study of "As You Like It,"* London, 1931.

WILLIAM EMPSON, *Some Versions of Pastoral*, New Directions, n.d., pp. 136–8.

B. IFOR EVANS, *The Language of Shakespeare's Plays*, Indiana, 1952, pp. 86–7.

W. W. GREG, *Pastoral Poetry and Pastoral Drama*, London, 1906, pp. 411–13.

G. WILSON KNIGHT, *The Shakespearian Tempest*, London, 1932, pp. 83–7.

THOMAS LODGE, *Rosalynde*, ed. W. W. Greg, London, 1907.

JOHN PALMER, *Comic Characters of Shakespeare*, London, 1946, pp. 28–52.

THOMAS MARC PARROTT, *Shakespearean Comedy*, New York, 1949, pp. 164–78.

J. B. PRIESTLEY, *The English Comic Characters*, London, 1925, pp. 20–42.

DONALD A. STAUFFER, *Shakespeare's World of Images*, New York, 1949, pp. 76–80.

DAVID LLOYD STEVENSON, *The Love-Game Comedy*, New York, 1946, pp. 198–207.

MARK VAN DOREN, *Shakespeare*, New York, 1939, pp. 151–60.

ENID WELSFORD, *The Fool*, New York, n.d., pp. 251–2.